PRAISE FOR AUTHENTIC S.A.L.E.S

"Great salespeople are trusted, authentic, humble problem-solvers who put the interests of their customers above their own. Travis shares practical ways to embody these values while leveraging your own God-given strengths."

—ALLEN MEACHAM, CHIEF REVENUE OFFICER, MEDICAL DEVICE IMPLANT

"My longtime friend Travis McCoy's book is a game-changer in the realm of solution-based selling. Travis played an integral part in my success as I transitioned from one career to another; he truly is the real deal. What sets Travis's book apart is its realistic approach. Beyond mere tactics, he delves into the meaningful aspects of the journey, like building trust, delivering value and earning loyalty. Through his expert guidance, you'll not only become a more effective salesperson but also experience transformative growth as an individual."

—RICH CLEMENTI, MILITARY VETERAN, UFC VETERAN, ENTREPRENEUR, COACH, CEO, HUSBAND AND FATHER

"As a former executive in the hospitality industry and now a small business owner in the automotive repair sector, I've consistently found Travis to be an invaluable resource for training and growth. My sales team has not only drastically increased their revenue goals but also experienced remarkable personal growth by implementing his process and finding their own style."

—MIKE FRIDGE, OWNER OF CHRISTIAN BROTHERS AUTOMOTIVE (FAYETTEVILLE, AR)

"Over the past 20 years, Travis is the only colleague with whom I've had the distinct pleasure of working both domestically and internationally on multiple occasions. I have observed him sell to doctors across diverse cultures around the globe. Even more impressively, I've seen him adeptly instill these traits into our international sales reps. Travis has a knack for quickly understanding a customer's perspective and authentically building rapport. He possesses the skills to influence customers and foster their self-awareness. I recommend this book to anyone looking to understand the mindset of one of the best medical device salespeople in the business."

—TOM COLLARD, SR DIRECTOR OF INTERNATIONAL BUSINESS DEVELOPMENT

"Nearly 20 years ago, I began my coaching journey with Travis. At the time, I was in marine manufacturing. With his guidance, I transitioned into medical device sales, where his mentorship was instrumental in helping me achieve P-club recognition multiple times. Travis possesses a unique clarity, discerning nuances that others often overlook. He simply gets it and assists those he coaches in identifying and addressing core issues effortlessly. I've often told him he should capture his wisdom in a book. I'm thrilled he's finally done it. For anyone in sales, this book promises to be a true eye-opener."

—ROBBIE LEININGER, TERRITORY MANAGER, MEDICAL DEVICES

"In the rapidly evolving tech landscape, clarity throughout the sales journey is paramount. To drive unparalleled sales outcomes, one must have a clear understanding of their position within the process. Awareness is how you achieve these results! I'm pleased to recommend a book on 'Sales Awareness,' authored by someone who not only mastered the challenges of being a rep but excelled beyond them."

—SHAWN TORRES, CEO, IN-TELECOM

"Travis has been a mentor and coach to countless award-winning sales professionals around the world. 'Authentic SALES' emphasizes nurturing flexibility and autonomy, enabling salespeople to become the most effective versions of themselves. Fast-paced sales environments demand adaptive and creative approaches. Travis McCoy's SALES process will equip your team for just that."

—DAVID JASINSKI, DIRECTOR SALES & MARKETING, MEDICAL IMPLANTS (EUROPE)

"People overthink sales, Sales reps are usually their own worst enemy. Travis does a great job simplifying the process for a rookie yet identifying important details for seasoned pros to focus on so they can take their revenue to the next level. Travis was the one rep I could count on. He would invest time and energy toward my success."

—BRAD BAKER, DISTRIBUTOR, MULTIPLE TIME "REP OF THE YEAR" WINNER

"Travis McCoy has been a vital professional mentor throughout the past two decades of my career. Under his thoughtful and expert guidance, my career has soared to heights beyond my wildest expectations. This journey has spanned B2B sales, surgical devices, capital equipment sales, and now includes selling surgical robots. Throughout it all, Travis's process has been consistently applicable."

—ANDREW C. ZERINGUE, SALES MANAGER, MEDICAL STARTUP

"Packed with practical principles and illustrated with compelling examples, Authentic SALES provides huge value for sales leaders at all levels. It's filled with strategies that can be implemented in both your business and personal lives. It's well structured for anyone regardless of experience, looking to become a stronger, more well-rounded sales individual. This book has helped make me a better sales leader and enabled my entire team to strengthen our game!"

—DONNIE MURPHY, NATIONAL SALES DIRECTOR OF MEDICAL DEVICES AND CAPITAL EQUIPMENT

"Travis McCoy nails it! He masterfully describes how being intentional with self-awareness can change human behavior to achieve customer acquisition through retention. Having read numerous books on selling over my 32 years in the financial services arena, most instruct you to sell 'their way.' In contrast, Travis guides you on how to sell 'your way.' He emphasizes staying authentic to create the ultimate trust and firmly believes in building lifelong relationships. This book is a must-read for anyone serious about connecting at the highest level, whether with clients, a team, or leading a family."

—RICK CANAMAR, THE CANAMAR GROUP, PREVIOUS IFBB PRO

"Great read about a very intentional sales process. The skills discussed in this book, such as discovering what the customer truly wants, has led to various individuals winning multiple sales awards at Fortune 100 companies, including myself. If winning at sales is what you want, read this book."

—MATT MAHONEY, MANAGER OF THE YEAR & MULTIPLE P-CLUB WINNER

"I've been in the medical business for nearly two decades and have participated in many sales coaching courses. Without question, Mr. Travis McCoy's SALES process stands out as the best I've ever encountered.

After the first SALES process training, led by Mr. Travis McCoy years ago, my peers and myself enthusiastically applied it. My colleagues universally expressed how well it aligns with their personal style.

Mr. Travis McCoy has been a friend, colleague, and mentor to me for many years. Each time he mentors me with the SALES process, I come away feeling incredibly empowered."

—TONI KOKKO, SENIOR ACCOUNT MANAGER, PRESIDENT'S CLUB WINNER, NORDICS

"It's never the brand. It's never the land. It's always the man. With Travis's customer-centric sales process, you will be that man or woman that makes a difference."

—TROY DUHON, OWNER OF PREMIER AUTOMOTIVE, FOUNDER OF GIVING HOPE FOOD PANTRY

"Travis's coaching and mentoring played a pivotal role as I transitioned from being an athlete to a medical device representative. Even now, as I sell surgical robotics, I implement the strategies he taught me. His emphasis on authenticity and efficiently identifying the core issues deeply resonated with me. This book is a must-read for anyone involved in solution-based selling."

—JAMIE VARNER, REGIONAL SALES MANAGER IMAGING, NAVIGATION, ROBOTICS, UFC VETERAN AND WEC WORLD CHAMPION

"Travis wasn't just an outstanding sales rep; he evolved into the best sales coach our organization has ever seen. His coaching and SALES process personally guided my transition from a Field Support Engineer to a President's Club-winning sales rep, equipping me to outperform seasoned competitors. This book is more than just strategy; it's a roadmap to finding your authentic sales voice. I truly hope my competitors never discover it!"

—CAMILLE JOUVAL, TERRITORY MANAGER, BRAIN IMPLANTS (EUROPE)

"Travis's SALES process transcends international borders, having proven its value by revitalizing our sluggish sales performance in Japan's challenging markets. His approach slices through cultural complexities, fostering growth by equipping our local sales reps with practical and effective sales skills. These methods are not mere theories; they're practical tools for achieving international success and delivering a lasting impact on revenue."

—HIROTO TAKAHASHI PHD, MEDICAL AFFAIRS & LIAISON TO KEY OPINION LEADERS, MEDICAL DEVICE (TOKYO)

"Working internationally with Travis allowed me to observe his sales process firsthand. I've noted its consistent success with customers and, more critically, its positive reception among sales reps. Travis has a gift for discerning user needs where others don't. 'Authentic SALES' is an absolute must-read, bridging the methodology gap present in many sales training manuals used by the best companies in the world…being true to *oneself.* Read it before your competition does!"

-BRAD OATES, ENTREPRENEUR, MULTILINGUAL, GLOBAL MARKETING AND SALES CONSULTANT, JOHNSON & JOHNSON TOP GUN SALES AWARD

AUTHENTIC SALES

SELLING WITH PURPOSE AND STRATEGY

TRAVIS MCCOY

STREAMLINE BOOKS

Published by Streamline Books
www.streamlinebookspublishing.com

Book Cover Design by **Hannah Crabb**

ISBN:
979-8-89165-053-4 (paperback)
979-8-89165-054-1 (hardback)
979-8-89165-055-8 (e-book)

CONTENTS

Preface xvii

Introduction xxiii

1. Changing Behaviors 1

2. Elite Professionals 15

3. What Selling Is (and What it is Not) 41

4. Connection and the Journey 59

5. Awareness Quotient 83

6. The S.A.L.E.S Process 115

7. Strategize 123

8. Articulate Your Message 145

9. Listen and Learn 171

10. Explore Emotions 195

11. Solidify 223

12. Stay Authentic 233

Afterword 241

Acknowledgments 243

About the Author 245

DEDICATION

I dedicate this book to my Beautiful Wife and loving family, whose values have shaped me profoundly.

PREFACE

I wrote this book with the intention of helping anyone who works in a sales capacity, or anyone in a non-sales role who has a solution they want to pitch or a vision they want others to join in on.

Over the past twenty-five-plus years, I have observed tons of companies and hundreds of sales individuals across multiple industries. I have seen them adopt stringent, non-conforming, ineffective sales processes, implemented through unrealistic simulated roleplay. When these sales individuals were eventually turned loose, I witnessed how quickly they abandoned these well-practiced techniques and resorted to a completely different style, full of bad habits. Their reasons for "going rogue" were completely understandable. These outdated techniques did not match the individual's style, personality, or the real-life situation. More often than not, when these individuals made a valiant attempt at using a new stringent sales process they ended up missing the mark, failing to capture their prospect's attention, unable to uncover core concerns or bring any real value to the interaction.

Throughout my career, I have wrestled with how to get people in the sales industry to understand the benefit of allowing their representatives more flexibility and autonomy. There is so much value in encouraging sales representatives to be more authentic during their sales interactions. My goal in this book is to present an adaptive system that allows the individual to stay true to themselves, tailoring the process to their strengths and resulting in a higher level of comfort in any given sales situation. The more comfortable you are with something, the more often you will do it. The more often you do it, the better you will be at it. The better you are at it, the more confident you will be in using it (not just in roleplay scenarios).

This leads me to the next question: Why do companies waste their money and risk their future revenue on ineffective sales training? The answer is simple: Change is hard. Sales culture evolves slowly over time. Most companies use a rigid sales process across their whole sales team, a process that lacks adaptability to differences in their reps' skill sets or style and flexibility to allow for audibles to be called when needed.

Often during corporate sales training, the continued use of these obsolete techniques are reinforced in a "Catch 22" situation. When sales managers observe individuals failing in roleplays, it reinforces the need in their minds to double down on the same, ineffective processes in an attempt to improve that rep's roleplay performance. They are ignoring the fact that performing the perfect roleplay in the *wrong* situation or at the *wrong* time will never help you close a deal.

Do not hear me wrong on this, sometimes working through failure is the best way to grow as a sales professional. I am all about having a growth mindset and stretching people out of their comfort zones to make them better. Research has proven over and over that an individual's belief is a larger indicator of growth potential. When reps follow a stringent sales process that they feel they are bad at and that will not help them, then there will be little to no self-improvement.

This is not an instructional book as much as it is a guide to purposefully and strategically navigating sales in complex scenarios throughout different industries. The process I am introducing is tailored around the rep, not the other way around. If you are in sales, I believe you will be able to receive something meaningful from this book, whether it's improving your closing average, growing your referrals, converting competitive accounts, or developing a deeper connection with your existing customers.

At the heart of this book lies the essence of communication and the profound act of helping, which are two pillars that form the bedrock of our lives. While the focus here is on sales, the principles and strategies discussed have far-reaching applications. Embrace them, and you won't just find success in sales but also in leadership roles, as a team member, and even in personal realms like parenting. This isn't just a guide to selling products; it's a manual to enrich relationships, to understand and be understood. Because, after all, the art of selling is intrinsically tied to the art of connecting. Dive in, and let's enhance not just our professional prowess but the quality of our interactions in every walk of life.

AUTHENTIC SALES

INTRODUCTION

Knock, knock.

"Hi, Travis, do I need my lawn mowed already?"

"No ma'am, not yet. I am starting another business. I'm painting house numbers on curbs so that when there's an emergency, police and firefighters will not drive right past your house. Since you have the nicest yard in the neighborhood, I really wanted your house to be my model home."

A naive eight-year-old lifts up his parents' Polaroid camera. The year is 1985, and I just made my first sales pitch, standing there on my neighbor's front porch full of confidence.

What Mrs. Hamilton does not yet realize is that her curb is getting painted one way or the other. The only question is whether or not this eight-year-old is going to do it for free or get paid for it. I truly believed her beautiful house would best showcase my painted numbers, not only would it make for a perfect picture, but it would likely help me sell to other houses because hers was the envy of the neighborhood.

Mrs. Hamilton smiles. "How much?"

That moment, standing on Mrs. Hamilton's front porch, was the moment I first realized that I was on to something, though I could not fully understand what it was at the time. It would take several years, spread across multiple industries, before I was able to fully comprehend the psychology behind this type of sincere selling. Ultimately, that is what led me to develop the system and strategies that would become *Authentic SALES*.

While it is widely accepted that sales is a numbers game, it would be a mistake to think that's all it is. To that eight-year-old boy holding a shoebox full of handmade stenciled numbers and a can of spray paint, each answered door and face-to-face interaction meant the world. I was forced to start my sales career with a low-volume, high-expectation mindset for two reasons. First, I was not allowed to ride my bike past the third stop sign. Second, I had already counted all the houses on my street and formulated my own quota, a quota that did not account for any rejections. It is amazing how meaningful each interaction will become when your prospects are limited and your closing ratio is critical.

How then, when there is so much pressure on a sale, can we avoid coming across as desperate? Often this need to close the deal in every interaction can lead to paralysis by analysis in the sales rep or raise suspicion in the potential customer. The ratio of interactions to closed sales differs from industry to industry, as well as from sales rep to sales rep, so there is no one-size-fits-all formula. Finding the right balance is key. No matter your situation, this book will focus on improving your batting average.

Here is what you should expect to gain from this book:

- **A sales process that will exemplify your strengths**
- **An improved closing percentage**
- **Enhanced customer experience and loyalty**
- **The key to unlocking endless referrals**
- **A way to prevent warm leads from stalling out**
- **Techniques to enhance prospecting and keep your pipeline full**

Be wary of any sales book that feels too difficult or unnatural to implement. This book is designed to be easy. What I share will mean something different to each reader, tailored to their individual style, because sales is not meant to be a paint-by-numbers process. We will focus on sharpening your awareness of your individual differentiators and how to lean on your unique strengths. In doing so, you will learn to sell from the heart, regardless of whether you are brand new to sales or a long-tenured sales professional trying to get back to the top of the leaderboard.

An old mentor of mine from my time at Edward Jones Financial once told me this: "Customers pick up on more than you think. So, if a sales process makes you uncomfortable and you do not believe in it, then your client will not believe in you. This is why reps struggle with strict sales processes." I found it difficult to argue with him then, and I feel the same way now.

I wrote this book because I want to help people find their style, their story, and their voice. I have spent decades observing the great reps across industries and across cultures, and the biggest thing I have learned is that there is not a consistent one-size-fits-all method for successful sales. Selling in a way that is authentic to you and focused on your customers is what matters most.

Sales is a great calling in life. It is an opportunity to help someone solve a problem faster or more efficiently, leaving them better than when you found them. I believe that the most driven and caring individuals should make up our global sales force in every industry. If you are in sales, you should care about the effect you're having on the people you're working with. You should care about doing it ethically (if you do not, this is not the book for you). You should care about impacting people for good.

I will not spend much time in this book talking about myself, except to share relevant examples. I want you to have an idea of who's writing this book, to understand that I have been in the sales trenches, just like you, for decades. The principles I have learned have come from observing sales reps all over the world, but also from my own experience.

So, here is a brief rundown of my sales resume. The experiences I have had over the years that shaped my perspective and made me who I am as a sales professional:

- My first sales "job" was the story I told to open this introduction: offering to paint address numbers on my neighbors' curbs. I also had a lawn-mowing business that I sold to those same neighbors.
- When I was about eleven years old, I started buying small motorcycles, fixing them up, and reselling them. I continued this all throughout high school.
- In college, I had a few non-sales jobs. I bartended, worked as a bouncer, and even worked as a (below average) DJ on the slower nights at a bar just off campus called Mickey's. Then, at the end

of my freshman year, I bought a house and rented out the extra rooms to a few of my fraternity brothers. The following year, I bought another house on the same street, and this led to me beginning to rent out houses to other students at my university.

- Toward the end of my sophomore year, one of my fraternity brother's father started sending us to an auto auction to buy inventory for his used car lot. Between my love for cars and the excitement of an auction, I was hooked, and I decided to get a dealer's license myself. I negotiated with a car detailing business to use half of their lot as the location of my own small used car dealership. From there, I started buying and selling cars. I usually had about three or four cars at any given time. It was my first big dive into real sales, and it helped finance the rest of my college education.
- As I got closer to graduation, I started slowing down my auto sales business because I wanted to gain some experience working for a bigger company to learn more about selling in corporate America. I started selling residential and commercial security systems, going door-to-door and working with customers face-to-face. It was a great chance for me to learn about prospecting and selling a product for a company that had their own sales strategy and marketing support. It also allowed me to learn from the more experienced sales reps that I worked with.
- After graduating college, I got my first full-time job with Rent-A-Center selling rent-to-own furniture. I was responsible for the entire process

from beginning to end, selling a customer a bedroom set or appliance in the showroom, negotiating price, verifying employment, structuring the payment process, delivering the furniture to their home, and installing it. If they were not able to pay, I was the one who came to collect. If they ultimately refused or were unable to pay, I was the one who had to repossess their furniture. It helped me see the entire process from end-to-end and gain a real appreciation for customers' experiences before, during, and after a sale.

- After Rent-A-Center, I worked in different sales roles and gained experience across a few different industries. I worked at Norwest Financial selling various financial products, Conseco Mortgage as a loan officer selling loans, Invivo Research selling vital sign monitors (capital equipment for hospitals), and Edward Jones Financial as a stock broker selling financial solutions and life insurance. Working across different industries helped me appreciate the different challenges sales reps can face, but it also helped me see similar foundational principles that are true across different types of sales.
- In 2004, I left Edward Jones to return to medical sales, and I landed a job with a startup company that was purchased a few months later by Boston Scientific, the company where I spent the bulk of my career. We launched our one and only product in mid-2004, a spinal cord stimulator implant. Since we were a small startup, selling our more expensive product entailed selling the

implanting physician, the financial decision-makers at the hospital, and the national buying groups they were contracted with. Then we had to educate the following: the patient, the hospital's billing department, OR staff, physician's clinic staff, referring physicians, and the patient's family. We also had to collect on past-due invoices. All this while fighting the competition. In my first full year of selling, I finished second overall in revenue for the entire company. The rep who finished first was taller, stronger, more polished, and smarter than me. It was pretty intimidating having to do role plays with him and especially after him (thank goodness we were not bonused off of role plays or I would have been broke). I refused to let roleplaying results dictate my sales career at Boston Scientific. So, I dug in and focused on what I did best, connecting with my customers, making their lives better, and focusing on outcomes. The next year, I crushed him. I finished as the top sales rep in the entire company, and continued on to set company records. In total, I was in the field selling for eleven years, was a President's Club winner ten times, had my territory cut six times, and was the number one revenue producer seven times. I worked hard for those accomplishments, but the number I am most proud of is "five", which is the number of junior reps I hired, trained, poured into, and watched them become President's Club winners themselves.

- In 2015, the President of my company asked me to move to an international role where I could make an impact at a larger scale by coaching our international sales reps on strategy and execution. For the next eight years, I got the privilege to work with sales individuals all over the globe, giving me the opportunity to observe and capture best practices from highly successful sales reps across different cultures and different financial landscapes. To learn what success looks like no matter what part of the world you are in or what type of customers you are selling to. More than anything, it was the biggest driver for me to create the method I am going to share with you in this book. I have been blessed with an opportunity to learn from a wide, diverse range of skilled sales professionals, and my goal in this book is to share what I learned with you in a way that will help you crush your sales goals and grow as an individual. I sold a ton when I was working as a rep, but it was not until I went international that I realized how much room I still had to grow. Whether you are a tenured sales rep or brand new to selling, I want to help you grow into the best version of yourself and be more successful than I was.

Before we dive in, I want to offer you a challenge and a promise. First, I want to challenge you to go into this book with an open mind. I might use examples or offer tips that do not feel specifically relevant to the industry you work in or the type of customers you work with. I might reference a product type that is different from what you sell, or even use the word "product" when what you sell is actually a service, technology, or something else.

Keep reading, stick with the process. Think intentionally about how to use the principles in your situation. I have never sold a "new car" in my career, but I have been able to better my game and grow my sales skills over the years by learning from a few of my friends in the "new car" industry, who happen to be amazing at retaining loyal customers (one being Josh, best man in my wedding, and another named Stephen, I'll talk more about him later in the book). The different sales techniques I used for the products I have sold in the past didn't have much in common with each other, but I always searched outside the box for those pearls of wisdom that would cross over and bring value. This mindset helped me grow and expand my perspective, and it opened me up to new approaches I could use with my own customers, no matter what I was selling. That is my challenge for you in this book: even if you encounter an example that doesn't seem to relate directly to your industry, look for that pearl. Find the takeaway that you can use to make yourself better.

Even if you are not in sales, think about how they might apply in your life or workplace. Leaders have to sell their vision, and good leaders do not just sell the vision one time, they revisit it often with various members of the team. Coworkers are always sharing and then selling new ideas to do something they believe to be different that will make a positive impact on the task or project at hand. Most small business owners do not consider themselves sales reps, but know they need to sell more of their product or service to grow their business. If you read this book with an open mind and willingness to look for the ways it applies to you,

I promise that it will help you grow, no matter your role or situation.

Second, my commitment to you is that I am going to practice what I preach in this book. I believe the sales approach I outline here can make you a better salesperson, and the foundation of all of it is caring about your customer above everything else. In the same way, what I care most about right now is you: your experience, your growth, your future success with your customers and as a sales professional in general. I want you to get something meaningful out of your time with this book.

I am not going to waste time selling it to you or explaining to you why it is better than all the other sales books. I am going to focus on giving you real value. By the end of chapter one, I will have shared with you the single most important behavior I have observed in every good sales rep I have worked with, the secret sauce to my sales approach so that even if you stop there, you will walk away with something valuable.

I hope you will not stop there, though. I believe what is in this book could change the way you look at sales for the better, help your customers feel like you truly value them as people, and make you a more successful salesperson. I hope you will read it, take it to heart, and use it to help your customer in more meaningful ways.

CHAPTER 1
CHANGING BEHAVIORS

IMAGINE THAT YOU COULD CHOOSE ANY SUPERPOWER TO MAKE yourself the best sales professional in the world. What would you pick?

If you take a minute to seriously reflect on this question, you will probably learn something about yourself. Think big, and while you are thinking, consider: What obstacles and resistance do you face when you are selling? How could you overcome them? Do you struggle with prospecting leads? Or with keeping leads engaged and excited until you convert them to customers? Or keeping your existing accounts loyal? Have you thought of a superpower yet?

I love asking this question in my sales training sessions. It gives me insight into the minds of the sales reps I am working with, and it helps them understand themselves better, too. Believe it or not, one of the most common answers I get, even from above-average sales reps, is the ability to be in two places at the same time. Not a bad answer. It tells me that they care about their customers, they are thinking about efficiency, and they understand the importance of solving multiple needs. However, it is not *the* answer. It shows me their mindset is reactive, not proactive.

Some of the more seasoned sales reps I have encountered have chosen mind-reading. Now we are getting somewhere! Having this level of awareness to know what your customer is thinking would obviously be enormously helpful in selling to them. If you know exactly what is on their mind, you will understand their needs and all the ways this product will improve their life, *allowing* you to articulate its benefits so well that *they* will be the ones wanting to speed up the sale so they can start using your product quickly.

Again, even though mind-reading is a good answer, it is not *the* answer. Play along with me in this scenario. I am a potential customer you are trying to sell to, and you have the power to read my mind. You are halfway through your presentation, and you decide to check in on what I am thinking about what you have shared so far. You listen to my thoughts, ready to hear my concerns and hesitations so you can amaze me by addressing them without me ever having to say them out loud.

When you read my mind, this is what you hear: "I really do need help, and it sure would be great if what he is saying was true. I just don't feel like I can trust him. I have never met him before, and he's trying to act like he knows my business. Hopefully, I can find a way to wrap up this conversation quickly."

There is no doubt that knowing what a potential customer is thinking would be a game-changer, but reading my mind doesn't help you very much if all you learn is that I do not trust you. If I do not trust that you have my best interests at heart, I am going to have a hard time believing that you are approaching this sale with any other motivation than just getting my business and taking my money.

That brings me to the real answer to this exercise, and I'll be honest, I started you off with a bit of a trick question. The best superpower you could possibly have as a sales professional is actually one you will not find in any comic book. Good news though, if you work at it and put what you learn from this book into practice, you can develop this superpower in real life. The superpower I am talking about, the one every sales professional should want, is immediate **trust**, to be trustworthy.

In sales, our ultimate goal is to influence a change in our customers' behavior. We want them to buy our product, obviously, but our best possible outcome is for them to change their pattern of behavior, to become loyal to us and our product, and to become an advocate on our behalf. Before any of that can happen, they need to have some sort of level of trust in us. They have to believe that we are out for their good, not our own, and that we truly care about what happens to them. Once we earn that trust, we can truly begin to help make their situation better.

The reality is that we do not live in a world where sales reps are graced with superpowers that make their jobs easier. (Probably a good thing, if we are being honest, controlling your customers' minds in real life would bring up just a few tiny ethical concerns.) Even the ability to earn your customers' trust is not something you are just granted by being struck by lightning or bitten by a radioactive spider. You have to work at it. So in our real, non-superpowered world, how do we achieve a higher level of influence over those that we are trying to serve, using only the abilities we currently have at our disposal?

If you can answer that question, you are well on your

way to leveling up your game as a sales professional. Ultimately, this is the question we are going to spend the rest of this book discussing. Our goal is to influence our customers to change their behavior in a way that will, in the end, benefit them as much as it benefits us. To understand how to do that, we need to start with understanding what motivates people to change their behavior in the first place.

WHAT INFLUENCES CHANGE?

If influence is our goal, then we first need to understand motivation. If trust is not present, what motivates people? Why do they do the things they do? Like the things they like? Buy the things they buy?

At the core, all human behaviors are essentially guided by three factors: positive emotion, negative emotion, or logic.

- **Positive emotion**: "Having this will make things so much better!" Think about the excitement of hearing about a new, amazing smartphone: seven-day battery life, no dropped calls, shatterproof screen, nearly unlimited storage. Your life is about to get better!
- **Negative emotion**: "I'm going to end up losing some serious revenue if I don't get a new phone ASAP!" Now think about the frustrations in having a really old smartphone? Imagine you are on a lengthy phone conversation with a customer, and right when you get to the most important moment of the call, the call starts breaking up. They can't hear you. You can't hear them. As soon as you find better reception, your phone

starts abruptly warning you "0% battery". Right as it starts to power down, you're trying to memorize their number to call them from another phone, but the cracks on the screen make it difficult to tell if the last number is a seven or a one. This phone has literally cost you money in the form of a lost opportunity, and you are sick of how many times it has messed things up for you.
- **Logic**: "This just makes sense." No emotion here. You don't really use your smartphone all that often, but your old one is paid off and it is time to get a new one. Your cell phone company is offering a good deal, and the phone you are looking at meets your needs. Making this purchase now just makes sense.

You can see how all three of these factors could guide someone in a decision, and they all play a role in most major decisions we make. (Note: financial motivations obviously play a role in decision-making, but those can fall under any of these three categories, depending on the emotions in that situation.) Which one do you think has the power to motivate a desired change in behavior the fastest?

This is another question I like to ask in my sales training sessions, and I asked it once to a room full of sales reps in Germany. They were very knowledgeable and passionate about the product they sold. In fact, they felt so strongly that their product was superior to its competition (which I agreed that it was) that they believed if a customer simply learned about its features, they would realize there was really no other choice. So, when I asked them what approach motivates a change in behavior the fastest, their response was almost unanimous: logic.

Unfortunately for these reps, and for all of us, that answer was (and still is) wishful thinking. It would be great if influencing behavior change was as simple as explaining why our product is the best and watching our highly intelligent customers sign on the dotted line. But that is not the way it works. To illustrate this, I asked those sales reps to think about their own personal purchases and big life decisions. What was the final straw for them leaving their last job? What pushed them over the edge to commit to a successful diet or exercise plan?

It was like watching a room full of light bulbs turn on all at once. Many of the reps smiled and acknowledged the same thing: almost all of those big personal behavior changes were motivated by negative emotions. They left their job because they had developed negative emotions toward their manager, their compensation plan, or lack of appreciation. They committed to stretching every day because their physical therapist told them it was the only way to avoid shoulder surgery, or to dieting because their family physician said if they don't get on a healthy diet immediately they will need to start taking medication for their type 2 diabetes.

Next, we turned our attention back toward their customers. They wanted to believe that their customers had the uncanny ability to remove emotions from their purchasing behaviors, but that is just not how we are wired as humans. We are emotional beings, and even when we are at our most rational, our emotions play a role in our thoughts and decision-making.

I asked the reps if they'd ever witnessed a customer making a snap decision about a product that they were not the ones selling, a choice to switch vendors quickly when the surgeon had not been actively looking to switch. Several raised their hands, and they each shared stories about what provoked their customers' quick change from one product to another. When we peeled back the layers and examined each scenario, it became obvious that the decisions in every single one of their stories had been motivated by a negative emotion, created either by disappointment with their current product/service or dissatisfaction with the rep who had sold it to them.

I then brought the attention back toward their business. We dissected some of their success stories and started to see where negative emotion participated in the conversion and sale. Again, this was a room full of solid sales reps who were selling their device with logic and positive emotion, but negative emotion attached to their competitor acted as the catalyst, like a nudge over the chasm. The negative emotion that was created organically, thanks to the competition, ignited the change toward the new and obvious solution this German team had ready to implement.

There's really no contest: the fastest approach to influence a change in behavior is through negative emotion. Sometimes, that can be a useful piece in the sales process, but it's also by far the riskiest approach. Selling with negative emotion is like playing with fire.

Here is why: if you become known as the sales rep who is constantly crying wolf or warning that the sky is falling, you will lose credibility the instant one of your predictions doesn't come true or your facts are found to be incorrect. If everything is a potential crisis, nothing is a potential crisis.

More importantly, if you become known as a harbinger of doom and negativity, who's going to be happy to see you? It is the same principle that applies anywhere else in life. If you are the family member who always reopens old emotional wounds at family get-togethers, your family probably will not be thrilled to be seated next to you. If you are the friend in the group who's always pointing out how bad things are, you might stop receiving invitations to group hangouts. If your goal is to form good relationships with your customers (hint: it should be), "that negative sales rep" is not how you want to be perceived.

One of the oldest sales mantras, one we will be talking about a lot more in this book, is "You buy from who you like." Consistently taking a negative approach is a foolproof way to ensure that you will not be liked. It jeopardizes your relationships, and it establishes a predictably negative environment every time you show up. It will brand you as negative. While it can capture your customers' attention, it is not going to help you gain the recurring revenue or referrals that lead to long-term success.

That is where positive emotion comes in. By helping your customer understand the positive impact your product would have on them, you are giving them the chance to be the hero. By using your product, they have a chance to not only solve a problem they have been struggling with, but to make everything even better than it was in the first place. It is your job to paint a picture for them of a world that gets significantly better when they are armed with your product or appropriately using your service.

Helping them see the positive potential of your product doesn't mean that they will be ready to purchase it immediately. Just because they can imagine a world where they are the hero doesn't mean that they are going to immediately walk out the door looking for dragons to slay. This is where my version of the 80/20 rule comes in: 80% positive emotion, 20% negative emotion. After you have helped them envision the best possible outcome of using your product, it is okay to spend some time helping them envision the possible negative outcome of *not* using your product. By this point, you have already helped them imagine the best that they can be, and once they have truly envisioned it for themselves, they will not settle for anything else.

This matters for a lot of reasons. If you truly care about your customers, you should want to see them succeed, but teaching them to run from their fear or frustration doesn't help them run toward the best version of themselves. Your job is to help them run in the correct direction, not just away from the negative, but toward what is truly best for them. To do that, you have to take time to listen to them, to understand what is important to them, find the core issue and what they want, then help them see how your product will transition them from a place of frustration to a place of positive impact.

It also opens up the possibility of a real, authentic relationship with your customer. Positive emotion may not work as quickly as a motivator as negative emotion, but it forces you to be truly tuned in to what your customer is thinking and feeling. "Quick" shouldn't be your goal anyway, you don't want quick transactions. You are striving toward something bigger, a strong relationship that withstands the test of time, a relationship that leads to a happy, loyal customer who champions your product or service, yielding lots of referrals and positive feedback. If that is what you want, you have to genuinely care about them. Let me tell you, when you genuinely care about someone, they will know it. They will trust you more, retain more of what you share with them, and be much more likely to stay connected to you long-term.

A REASON TO RETURN

In the introduction, I promised you that in the first chapter of this book I would share with you the single most important thing that I have observed in the best sales reps I have worked with. Drum roll, here it is: in all my observations, all my ride-alongs, all my personal experiences across different scenarios, different industries, and very different cultures (spanning five of the seven continents), I have not observed anything more powerful or more important than creating a *meaningful and interesting Reason to Return.* If you put this book down after the next few paragraphs and never pick it up again, you will still walk away with this. If you put it into practice, you will drastically increase your ability to help customers and your own income.

Your main goal should not be "close the deal" every single time you meet with a customer. There is something more powerful to strive for every time you have an interaction with a customer or potential customer, and it is simple: giving yourself a meaningful and interesting reason to go back. In sales, the only way to make sure you lose the game is to no longer be in the game. Focusing on and achieving a Reason to Return makes the game you are playing infinite; it keeps putting time back on the clock for you to try again. It is like eating an elephant, one bite at a time.

If you are a baseball fan, or if you have seen the movie *Moneyball,* you are probably familiar with Billy Beane and his innovative philosophy with the Oakland A's in the early 2000s. Beane knew that his team could not compete financially with larger market teams to sign the biggest-name players, so he had to find a different way to win. So, he decided to focus his team's strategy on the first thing a baseball player needs to do to score a run: getting on base.

They didn't care about home runs, steals, or anything else. They focused on signing players who could make it to first base on a regular basis. Beane knew that his team didn't need to lead the league in home runs to win games, they just needed to keep each inning alive and stay in the game. It worked: in 2002, Oakland won 103 games, tied for the most in the American League. They focused on staying in the game, and they won a lot.

We will go deeper on creating interesting and meaningful Reasons to Return later in the book. For now, file this away, there is nothing more important than making sure that each sales call with a customer is not your *last* sales call with that customer. For this to happen, your Reason to Return needs to be interesting and meaningful to them, and again, they need to like you, or at least want to see you.

That brings us back to selling with positive emotion. When you help someone envision a world in which they are the hero, they are going to want to live in that world. When you take their concerns seriously and show real interest in understanding them, they are going to know you are being genuine. When you care about what is truly best for them and they not only notice it but feel it, then they will start to build real trust in you. They will be glad to have you back and answer your follow-up phone calls.

Not every swing can result in a home run, but if you hit enough singles by giving yourself meaningful and interesting Reasons to Return, eventually you are going to light up the scoreboard.

AUTHENTIC SALES

When my son played tee-ball, I coached his team. I was on the track team in college, so I thought, who better than me to help him learn to run the bases faster? He might not be a master of the glove or the bat yet, but with just a little work, he could be motoring around those bases. So, I worked with him on his form. I taught him to stride like my old teammates did. We practiced it over and over, and he was ready for the big debut of his new, 100-meter dash technique, and when my wife finally saw it…she told me I was not allowed to coach him anymore because I had made him look completely ridiculous when he ran.

The style of running I tried to teach my son didn't work for him. It didn't fit his build or his style. He worked hard and tried to do exactly what I told him to, but ultimately I was trying to force him into something that didn't fit his body type or his natural ability. After encouraging him to revert back to what felt natural and running drills for him like that, his speed increased and more importantly, he looked normal.

I called this book *Authentic SALES* for the same reason. If you are willing to put in the work to reach customers and you are committed to caring about their needs more than anything else, then you have what it takes to succeed in sales. I am not here to drill some one-size-fits-all sales process into your head. I am not here to teach you how to sell exactly like I do. A huge piece of succeeding in sales is learning to understand yourself better, your strengths, your weaknesses, what feels natural for you and what doesn't. What works well for me might not work the same for you, and that is okay.

That is why you need a sales process that allows your natural strengths to shine through, not one that forces you into a box that doesn't work for you. I wrote this book to equip you with an algorithm that will work with your skill set, that you can adjust around your strengths. A solid framework that you can customize to find your own style and delivery.

There are lots of great sales processes out there, but what you will find different in this book is a sales process that anyone can tailor to their own strengths and style. It will help you succeed as a sales rep for the long haul, and it will go a long way toward building a foundation of trust with your customers. I am not here to teach you to sell my way. I am here to help you unlock the best version of selling *your* way.

CHAPTER 2
ELITE PROFESSIONALS

In the 2007 NFL Draft, the Oakland Raiders selected JaMarcus Russell with the first overall pick. The Raiders had every reason to believe that Russell was going to turn things around for their franchise. He was a five-star recruit out of high school, he was named first-team all-SEC his final season in college at LSU, and he was an incredible athlete, bigger and stronger than most quarterbacks, with a cannon for an arm. He had all the talent and physical tools to become a Hall of Fame NFL quarterback and lead the Raiders to the Super Bowl.

But things went south almost immediately. Instead of hitting the ground running, Russell was not happy with the contract the Raiders offered him. He thought he deserved more money as the first overall pick, so he refused to sign, missing all of training camp and even the team's first regular season game. It was an omen of how the remainder of Russell's NFL career would go. After choosing him with the first overall pick, the Raiders cut Russell after just three seasons. He finished his career with 18 touchdowns and 23 interceptions, and the Raiders' combined record in the three seasons Russell was on the team was 14-34. (You probably do not need to be a football fan to know: that is not good.)

Russell had natural physical gifts that most football players could only dream about. His attitude, mindset, and work ethic held him back. Three of the thirteen players selected immediately after Russell are now in the Hall of Fame. Russell had the talent to be the fourth. Instead, his NFL career ended after three disappointing seasons. Simply put, he didn't reach his potential because he was not willing to put in the work and take on the mindset he needed to improve.

Meanwhile, while Russell was missing games as an NFL rookie, there was another quarterback who had already been dominating the league since he entered it in the year 2000. This quarterback didn't come highly touted out of college, and he was not selected in the NFL draft until the sixth round. In fact, 198 players were picked before him. He didn't have out-of-this-world physical traits, but what he did have was hunger to keep getting better, and to do whatever he had to do to win.

While JaMarcus Russell was missing his team's first game on his way to three disappointing seasons, this player had already won three Super Bowls and was on his way to a career with seven Super Bowl titles, five Super Bowl MVPs, and three NFL MVPs. The first of those NFL MVPs came in the year Russell was drafted (2007), and the second came in his first year out of the league (2010).

If you know anything about football, you have probably figured out that the player I am talking about is Tom Brady, almost universally regarded as the greatest quarterback in the history of football. The thing that most separates JaMarcus Russell's career from Tom Brady's is the same thing that separates sales professionals who succeed from those who fail or flame out: an elite mindset. Tom Brady approached his game from day one with the mindset of an elite professional. He worked hard, he practiced with intentionality, and he never, ever stopped looking for ways to get better. If you want to grow to be the very best you can be as a sales rep, that is the mindset you need to have, too.

It is easy for sales reps to fall into the trap of thinking they have it all figured out because they've been selling for such a long time. Sales individuals are the professional athletes of the corporate world, some continue to improve and some plateau and fade away. If you want to move to the next level, you have to be willing to take on the same mindset as elite professional athletes, hungry to grow, learn, improve, lean into your strengths, and be aware of your weaknesses.

So before we move on to the nuts and bolts of a successful sales approach, I want to talk about six traits that all elite professionals share, and why they are important to you in your sales career. Your mindset is where everything starts. If you get it right, it can lead you to becoming the very best version of yourself as a sales professional.

HUMILITY

Widely regarded as the greatest director of all time, Steven Spielberg secured his place in film history by smashing records and winning awards in all sorts of categories. He won the title of highest-grossing film ever with *Jurassic Park,* and then in that same year he released *Schindler's List* and then later *Saving Private Ryan.*

If Spielberg had only made those three films in his career, he would still get my vote as the best ever. Yet, if you pay attention to his work over the years, from *Jaws* to *E.T.* to

Lincoln, you will notice that he is always evolving, finding new ways to grow his craft, always branching out and trying different things. His approach is so varied that it is difficult to even describe his "style" of filmmaking.

How does someone on the top of their game learn something new, or even find the desire to? The answer is simple: humility. Steven Spielberg has given credit multiple times to young filmmakers, expressing how he learns more from young filmmakers than any other source. Their audacity and creativity inspired him to try new tricks and push the limits of directing. He is constantly looking outside himself, believing that the people around him have something to teach him and there are always ways for him to continue to grow.

No matter how good we are, there will always, always be someone better, who's more creative or more efficient. Even if you reach the pinnacle of your profession and you are the best in the world, there will always be someone who has done it longer, or someone who has had more success with a certain approach, or someone with keen awareness and can identify your weaknesses. There will always be room to learn and grow. Recognizing that is one of the biggest keys to becoming the best sales professional you can be.

If you want to really test your humility, ask yourself this: do you believe you can learn something from the newest sales rep on your team? Robbie Leininger is an extremely successful medical device sales rep that I had the privilege of working with for over fifteen years. Robbie started off as a junior sales rep. It was obvious from day one that he possessed more drive and humility than the senior rep he worked for, and within months, Robbie was as technically sound as his boss.

For the next several years, I never heard Robbie express what we all knew to be true: that he should be the senior rep. He just worked hard, took everything in that he could, and pursued additional mentoring and coaching to improve his skill set. Well, it paid off, patience and a grateful heart will often make things right, and that is exactly what happened for Robbie. It was not long before Robbie became a senior rep and was on stage receiving the first of many President's Club awards. A few years later, he finished number two in revenue out of all the reps worldwide.

I interacted with Robbie often, including monthly coaching calls. We would also spend time together at cadaver labs, conventions, new rep trainings, and company functions. Robbie showed up at every single one of these events with pure humility, listening to other people's stories of trials, errors, and victories. He engaged with them, congratulating them on hard-fought wins and listening to understand the meaningful details of what got them there. The coolest part is that most of these reps had half the revenue Robbie did. Some were just out of training. Most reps wouldn't even give the time of day to a new rep fresh out of training, but not Robbie. He felt that there is always a possibility to learn from someone, no matter their tenure or experience. Observing him interact with junior reps was humbling and eye-opening for me. Honestly, it changed me. I believe this mindset shaped Robbie into the leader and sales rep he is today, and it allows him to be authentic as he engages with his customers, believing that he will learn something from them too.

Humility is important in just about every aspect of sales. It helps you stay open to coaching, to fine-tuning your approach and continuing to learn. It helps you connect with customers and truly listen to their needs, rather than assuming you know them better than they know themselves. It helps you recognize when you fall short and use it as a growth opportunity.

Sir Dave Brailsford took over as head of Great Britain's professional cycling program in 2002. When he took over, British cycling had experienced almost nothing but failure. Only one Olympic gold medal in 76 years. Brailsford was determined to change that, he brought with him a new perspective and a strategic approach. His theory was that the team could grow and become a serious threat to the other teams by working to improve each element of their cycling technique by 1% increments. If they did this over time, he reasoned, those small improvements would eventually become big ones.

Brailsford was right. At both the 2008 Beijing Olympics (only six years after Brailsford took over) and the 2012 London Olympics, Great Britain won seven out of ten possible gold medals in track cycling, and British cyclists won the Tour de France six out of seven years from 2012-2018. Brailsford is now renowned for his "Marginal Gains Approach," which focuses on fine-tuning and always looking for ways to improve, especially if they seem small.

Examples of similar kinds of fine-tuning pop up all throughout history, from advances in math, science, and engineering to the evolution of athletic approaches like swing styles in golf and baseball, because it works. I didn't write this book to tell you to completely reinvent yourself. Instead, by fine-tuning your strengths, you can take those strengths to the next level. By building on the things you already do well, you can stay true to your foundation and grow to be the best version of yourself. Growth with an approach like this takes real, genuine humility.

Humble bragging is not humility if anyone is wondering. I observed the interviewing and hiring for a sales manager at a very impressive telecommunications company with over $15 million in annual revenue. This company was highly regarded, not only because of their financial success but also their excellent customer service. The root of this success came from excellent leadership by the company's two owners and their wives, a solid team of four who were (and still are) pure of heart and who I have a massive amount of respect for.

When I met this new sales manager, I immediately understood why the owners had been excited to hire him. On the surface, he seemed like everything you'd want in a leader for your sales team. He was very confident, and he said everything you would want a sales manager to say. He went on and on about his humility and how he was always open to hearing good ideas from his team. He said all the right things, but to me, something seemed off. It was obvious that he was extremely book smart, regurgitating quotes from leadership books that he memorized. There was just no substance in the conversations as you moved further and further from the talking points he led with. His stories didn't show any evidence of follow-through or perseverance. When you are interviewing for a job in sales, you are selling yourself, and the only warranty you have to offer is your character. Just like with products we sell, making outlandish claims and overpromising will always raise suspicion and bite you in the end. For the interviewee, it's all about reading the fine print.

Well, two weeks after he started, I got together with him for dinner and quickly realized it was all a charade. He was full of confidence, but it was false confidence, built on other people's experiences, with no real understanding of how to strategize or even execute someone else's strategy. Wait, it gets worse. He was fake-humble. His "I am always open to good ideas" was as fake as a Rolex on Craigslist. He said he wanted to listen and learn, but his actions showed that he sincerely believed he was better than everyone else. I could tell he was destined to flame out, and he did. The owners tried coaching him on several occasions, but he consistently ignored them because he thought his limited sales experience was superior to theirs. His lack of humility was his downfall.

No matter where you are in your sales journey, humility is everything. It can help you grow your way from mediocre to good, from good to great, and from great to elite. Keep in mind, even the most elite professionals realize that they always have room to grow, that everyone, even those with less experience, has something to teach them. If you can take on that mindset as a sales professional, you are on your way to greatness.

STRENGTHS AND WEAKNESSES

When he was already well into his career, UFC fighter Michael Bisping suffered an injury to his right eye. Bisping saw a doctor, and in Bisping's words, "just about everything that could go wrong with my eye, did go wrong". He eventually lost sight in his right eye completely.

Bisping understood the risks of continuing to fight with one good eye. His doctor emphasized to him that if anything happened to his other eye, he'd be completely blind, but he didn't want to stop. He was so determined to continue on his journey to become the Middleweight Champion of the World that he even bluffed his way through vision tests so each state-commissioned fight doctor would clear him to fight.

He obviously understood that his right eye was now his biggest weakness, so Bisping strategized accordingly. He never let anyone, especially his opponents, know that he only had one good eye. From that point on during his fights, he always circled to his good eye and never let his opponent circle to his bad eye. He clearly understood his biggest weakness, but he found a way to work around this insanely large weakness and lean solely on his strengths.

It worked, Bisping fought eleven times with his secret weakness, winning almost all of them, and ultimately becoming the UFC Middleweight Champion. He understood himself well enough that he was able to play to his strengths, even though his biggest weakness would have ended anyone else's career.

Some people have the discipline to work so hard on one of their weaknesses that it becomes a strength (assuming that weakness is not something permanent like blindness in one eye). If this happens to be the case for you, I commend you, but just know that is not the primary focus of this book. For the rest of us mere mortals, myself included, it is important to become aware of our strengths so we can polish them, and of our most detrimental weaknesses so we can avoid them. There have been numerous times in my own career when I went into a sales call without awareness of my own weaknesses, and that led me to take the wrong approach in the call. Thanks to securing a Reason to Return, I was able to salvage some of those trainwrecks.

Understanding your strengths and weaknesses will help you engage with your customers in a positive way that feels natural for you. They will be able to tell that you are being your authentic self, and that will build trust. It is much easier to sustain a sales approach over time if it's one that is built on things you are naturally good at, as opposed to banging your head against the wall over and over again to try to improve in an area that doesn't come naturally. An elite professional can separate themselves from the field with just a 1-2% improvement in an already existing strength, but they may not improve their standing against their competition at all by solely working to improve a weakness.

Over the past 15 years, I've coached tons of junior reps working to become senior reps, and I've coached senior reps who wanted to flat-out sell more. All of them were capable, willing, and determined to take their skills to the next level. I would always start by asking them if they wanted to work on a weakness to make them a more well-rounded sales rep, or if they'd rather fine-tune what they're already good at to become an expert in that area. It's like flipping a coin: 50% pick improving their weakness, and 50% pick fine-tuning their strengths. I'm still trying to find a trend to see if I can predict who will select strength and who will select weakness. I did find trends in my next observation. This is where things really got interesting. One-hundred percent of the individuals who focused on improving strengths achieved the following three markers:

1. Continued to demonstrate improvement over a six-month period.
2. Verbally acknowledged their improvement.
3. Applied their enhanced skillset on a regular basis.

Only 10% of the individuals who focused on improving

their weaknesses achieved all three of these markers for their weaknesses at the end of six months.

Because this was not a study, I was able to have casual conversations with these reps about their improvement or lack thereof, observe them in action on sales calls, and ask how they felt about the strength or weakness they were trying to improve. This interaction led to me drawing my own conclusion on the outcomes I was observing. To put it simply, people like working on activities they believe they are good at. People may want to improve a weakness, but they have a predetermined dislike toward their weakness, which reduces their willingness to actually work on it. Generally, people enjoy measuring the slow progression of a strength, but they're unhappy measuring the same slow progression in the improvement of a weakness. I believe their personal expectations play a role in the happiness of results.

Apparently, I am not alone in my observations, Harvard Business Review wrote an article with a similar conclusion. They also quoted a study that Gallup conducted on workplace performance improvement. They structured the study on the same premise, but focused on performance teams in a business. At the end of the day, both their academic study and my anecdotal "research" led to the same conclusion: working to fine-tune a strength is more satisfying and effective for most people than working to improve a weakness. Therefore people are more willing to put out additional effort toward improving a strength and see it through on their own without a coach or manager pushing them.

That said, if you want to work on your weaknesses and measure your improvements, do it! I think it is a great and wise goal and also a good investment of your time. Just keep in mind it is also wise to avoid using it in a professional setting until you have made a significant improvement in it. Just envision a surgeon wanting to perform surgery prior to being fully competent on the instrumentation needed.

To do any of this well you have to grow in your understanding of yourself. Overall awareness, including self-awareness, is one of the most under-appreciated elements of successful sales, so much so that we will be focusing on it specifically in an upcoming chapter. If you understand yourself, you will be able to lean into your strengths and approach your weaknesses with intentionality. The sales process I am going to lay out in the latter half of this book is one that you can easily tailor to your own strengths and away from your weaknesses to make it exactly the right fit for who you are.

EXPERIENCED MENTORS

There are two ways to learn most things in life: from your own experiences or from the experiences of others.

For most of my life, I have gravitated toward learning most of my lessons through my own experience, lots of trial and error, lots of learning from my (many) mistakes. This pathway can work, you just have to be able to stomach the losses, make fast corrections, and have natural awareness. Most people who head down this route don't do it with directionality. They usually find themself on this difficult pathway because of stubbornness or lack of knowledge. Even though "losses are lessons," they are not necessary to be successful. Now that I train and coach sales reps, I see how the journey I took can be drastically shortened for anyone who is simply humble enough to learn from someone else's mistakes.

Many elite professionals believe they can do it on their own, and that is not a bad thing. In many cases, it is probably true, and that level of self-confidence is huge for anyone trying to achieve high-level success. However, we will never become the best version of ourselves without opening ourselves up to others to step in and influence us. You might be able to do it on your own, but you will be able to do it even better if you have help.

Five years into his NFL career, Patrick Mahomes has already led the Kansas City Chiefs to three Super Bowl appearances, two of which they won. He's won league MVP twice, Super Bowl MVP twice, and he's been voted to the Pro Bowl every season that he's started. He's already considered a Hall of Fame quarterback. So you'd expect that when Patrick Mahomes entered the league as a rookie, he took the league by storm, right?

Wrong. The Chiefs correctly believed they had found their franchise quarterback when they selected Mahomes with the tenth pick of the 2017 NFL Draft. Although they already had a starting quarterback on their roster: Alex Smith, who had played in the NFL for many years. Smith was not a future Hall of Famer like Mahomes, but he had success in the NFL and was a steady hand that guided the Chiefs back to winning football after years of mediocrity. Mahomes spent the entire 2017 season backing up Smith, learning from how he approached the game and growing his own game by leaps and bounds in the process. When Smith was traded after the 2017 season, Mahomes took over as quarterback, and he hasn't looked back since, except to acknowledge what an influence Smith had on him. Mahomes has said many times that Alex Smith helped him develop into the quarterback he is today, crediting Smith many times for teaching him how to approach the game the right way and be the kind of leader a team needs their quarterback to be.

If you are reading this book, you are already heading in the right direction. You bought it because you want to improve, sell more, increase your revenue, make more money, and ultimately hit your personal goals. Well, my goal through this book is to do just that, to share what I have learned around the globe from the best of the best then help you implement it. Envision yourself receiving a long-awaited and hard-earned award on stage, and immediately afterward, a young rep who admires you (and possibly wants to dethrone you) asks, "How do you sell so much?" If you are like me, that question is extremely difficult to answer with a casual response and in some cases difficult to answer altogether. Sometimes, as reps, we are so engulfed with the actions of selling that we do not see the plays we are running. In this book, I will also help bring awareness to your actions so that one day you can elegantly answer that question and really make an impact mentoring other reps looking to grow.

KNOW YOUR COMPETITION

For years, my biggest competition was a medical device rep named Kevin. Selling against Kevin pushed me to be my best. Time and time again, I would watch Kevin deliver excellence to physicians and patients, focusing on outcomes and changing lives for the better. If Kevin was involved, you knew the surgery was going to run smoothly and be executed correctly. Early on, I could not find a weakness in his armor to exploit. Everyone needs a "Kevin" to get them fired up in the morning and to give them drive in the evening to knock on one more door, make one more call, write one more thank-you. Kevin was the Larry Bird to my Magic Johnson, or better yet, the Katie Kuric to my Diane Sawyer.

Kevin was the first competitive rep in my career to take business back after I had essentially won the business. So, it is safe to say when I heard his name mentioned in an account it captured my attention. Even though we despised each other and went as far as refusing to acknowledge one another when we crossed paths, I had total respect and learned a ton from Kevin over our five years of intense battling.

Kevin and I sold spinal cord stimulators, implantable devices that deliver a customized electrical waveform to the spinal cord stopping the pain signal to the brain. Outcomes were very dependent on the physician's skill level in placing the leads as well as the rep's skill level in understanding the patient's physiological response to the electrical current being delivered and their state of pain.

I worked for a startup. We received FDA approval just months after I was hired. Even though we had the new, shiny toy to sell, we didn't realize what we were up against as we entered a complex marketplace against a Fortune 100 company that had 90% of the market share in our industry. This company had pretty much invented this space, and they trained all the physicians who presently implanted spinal cord stimulators. The reps were good too, all of them able to perform the procedure on a cadaver by themself. As for me, I was up against Kevin, one of their top reps, a multiple-time President's Club winner, a seasoned rep who knew the business backward and forward and could articulate that knowledge in his sleep.

This guy was good, the physicians and patients loved them some Kevin. However, the hospital and clinic staff?

Not so much. So while he focused on the doctors, I took the other route, doing "lunch and learns" with the staff. The staff might have been learning about new technology, but I was the eager student, learning about everything Kevin did and said while he was in the clinic or in the operating room. The staff shared two things with me that were very interesting. Before I share them, keep in mind that Kevin had 100% of the business in his accounts and 90% of the market overall. These accounts were the definition of loyal customers.

The hospital staff said every single time Kevin showed up, he would start babbling about something new in pain medicine to the physician. They said that somehow, he would learn things about the pain medicine specialty before anyone else, things like new codes, publications, new indications, best practices, new drugs, or chiropractors moving to town. The way the staff described it didn't make this approach sound all that impactful, so I asked how the physicians received these meetings with Kevin and the information he shared. The staff said they loved it, the physicians looked forward to him coming in, and they gave him 100% of their attention when he would share something. They even described how Kevin didn't waste time with small talk. He would enter, walk right past the staff, and give his intel to the doctor like a soldier returning from a mission to debrief their commanding officer.

It had never dawned on me just how powerful it can be to bring something of value on every single visit. All the sales trainings I had participated in emphasized on uncovering information about your customer. We were taught that aside from a demo here or there, the real value in a sales call was you learning more about the customer so that you can better serve them or sell them. Kevin's approach was completely different. He was never viewed as a "sales rep" to these physicians. They all viewed him as a "consultant," even a "proctor" in some cases. Kevin was more focused on teaching first, then learning second.

In the end, Kevin turned out to be human. He had a flaw in his strategic approach: he was all or nothing with the decision-makers. He was hyper-focused on being efficient and giving 100% of himself to the decision-maker, but he underestimated the influence support staff has and how their actions can influence the ending of a story. After Kevin left the territory, selling got boring for a while, and I had to remind myself that I did the right thing by taking his accounts and forcing him into the next chapter of his life.

These days, Kevin and I are very close. We are even in the same men's Bible study. In fact, one Wednesday morning Kevin showed up with a memorized Bible verse, Proverbs 27:17, which says, "As iron sharpens iron, so one person sharpens another." Where would we be, he asked, if we didn't have people in our lives to sharpen us, to help us grow and become the best versions of ourselves?

It was almost like he knew I was writing this chapter. What Kevin doesn't realize (and what I do not plan on telling him) is that when we were selling against each other, he was the iron that was sharpening me. He was by far my toughest competitor, the one that forced me to raise my game and be the best version of myself. (Do not bother sharing this with him, if Kevin ever reads this book, I will say this paragraph was just one long typo.)

On a serious note, I urge you to find someone to compete with, either for fun within your company or in a more serious way with someone outside your company. We all need to be challenged to grow.

When Kevin left his position, he was replaced by a rep with a very different approach. The new rep was very relationship-focused. He wanted everyone in the office and hospital to enjoy his company. This was the exact opposite of Kevin. If the patient was getting good outcomes and the surgery went off without any issues, then Kevin would be just fine with you not smiling behind his back.

The new rep was such a relationship person that he would even use his personal relationships to help convert sales. He had been roommates in college with a well-known NFL quarterback, and he let everyone know it. It was hard to blame him. This connection was an easy way to spark interest with anyone who had any interest in football. He sometimes even alluded to the possibility that he could make an introduction. It was a unique tactic, and it got people to pay attention to him pretty quickly.

The problem was it made him completely predictable and one-dimensional. That made my job easy. I knew that mentioning his quarterback friend was this rep's signature move, so I got out ahead of him. When I knew I was selling against him, I'd make sure to say, "Oh, has he told you that he knows a certain famous quarterback yet? No? Time him and see how long it takes him. His standing record is at the VA Hospital, six and a half minutes on his very first conversation with the doctor."

Over time it became obvious that he was more concerned with making his customers happy than he was with making them better. He could have leveraged his relationships to implement new surgical best practices or new industry breakthroughs. Even as a relationship-focused rep, he had so much more potential if he had just focused on improving his customer's situation by focusing on better outcomes, he could have helped so many more patients. He had a different game plan, one that prevented him from reaching his full potential. He never leveraged his strength to benefit others, and because of that he never presented the same level of challenge as Kevin.

Knowing your competition matters. Sometimes you will find an easy weakness to exploit, and other times you will be humbled by how good they truly are. Either way, knowing the people you are competing against will help you grow as a sales professional and better understand how to communicate well with your customer. Understanding who you are selling against is just one more piece of helping your customer choose the product (and the sales rep) that's truly best for them.

One final note: not every sales rep who you see as your competition will actually work for your competitor. You might be able to think of someone right now who works for the same company as you, who you desperately want to outsell. Less of an Alex Smith vs. Patrick Mahomes dynamic, and more of a Steve Young vs. Joe Montana situation, where two great sales professionals are competing for the chance to be the best on the same team. If this is true for you, use it. Respect this person as your colleague, but if wanting to beat them drives you to work hard, improve your game, and go the extra mile for your customers, lean into it. There is nothing wrong with wanting to beat the best, especially if it brings about the best outcomes for your customers in the process.

INTENTIONAL PRACTICE

It is easy to assume that if we understand something well and do it a lot, we will get better at it. Now if that were the case, every taxi driver in America would be ready to make the jump to NASCAR. Many taxi drivers really do believe they are professional drivers. They may not actually believe they are NASCAR-caliber, but they believe with all their hearts that they are better drivers than you or me. As for anyone who has spent time in taxis knows that assertion is debatable at best. If you take into consideration the hours they've logged behind the wheel, it is pretty clear that experience alone does not make you great.

When you do something a lot, you are naturally getting practice time in. That does not make a single bit of difference unless you are practicing with *intention*. Have you established a baseline for your strengths and your weaknesses? Do you have a way to measure them? Are you fully aware of your strengths and weaknesses and what to focus your time on improving? Do you believe you can improve them? Can you envision them at your full potential? Or are you just going through the motions?

It is easy to overlook this part of your growth as a sales rep. If you want to grow, if you want to become the best version of yourself you can be, you can not leave it all to chance by thinking more sales calls alone will make you better. You will not observe improvement through mere repetition. You need to grow your awareness of yourself and where you need to improve, measure those improvements over time (we will talk more about that in a later chapter), and use that information to guide your time so you can practice well.

At one of my son's track meets, I volunteered to retrieve and throw back each discus as the athletes threw them. (Not a job for the easily distracted.) As I watched all the high schoolers get their warm-up throws in, it was obvious who the thrower to beat was. Even though his discus was sailing 10 feet past everyone else's, something was off. His technique was solid except for one thing: he was not getting enough rotation with the discus.

So, I shared with him between heats that if he pulled all the way through with his middle finger, he would increase the rotation on his discus. I was a NCAA Division One thrower in college, and I had actually thrown the discus on the same field where this meet was being held. He tried my suggestion during the warm-ups right before the finals, and his two practice throws looked great, he gained another 15 feet on both. Then he stepped into the ring for a real throw. He put everything he had behind it…and his throw looked horrible. It was his worst of the day.

I felt awful. I may have been technically correct in my advice, but I had completely messed up this kid's final throws. He still won, but it never feels good for your last throw of the day to be your ugliest. I learned a lesson that day: never mess with someone's swing in the middle of a game. I should have waited until the end of the meet to share that with him, allowing him to practice it on his own time.

The same is true about trying to hone your sales skills under the "bright lights" of a sales call. Have awareness and practice new material in a controlled environment. If you are presenting new information from a sell sheet, practice doing so over and over before you do it in front of a customer. If you have an upcoming demo with a new product, practice in front of a mirror. Better yet, record it and watch it back.

Take time to visualize the perfect sales call, your approach, how you want the customer to respond, everything that leads to the perfect ending scenario. Slow the scene down. Think about surprises that might come up, different curve balls your customer might throw at you, and how you will respond. Evaluate your own performance. Are you being who you want to be? Are you focusing on the customer and their needs? It might seem trivial to some, but this kind of visualization can be a powerful way to hone your mental game and equip yourself for success.

You can also practice in everyday scenarios with your friends and family. The fundamentals of how you approach a customer in sales are really no different from how you would approach anyone who you are trying to help by understanding their situation and guiding them through a difficult decision. It could be as simple as picking a restaurant to eat at, or a little more difficult by helping someone stay on a diet, or extremely important like helping a loved one make life-altering decisions associated with a toxic relationship.

We are going to get into the steps of the process later in the book, but until then, remember this: you need to understand someone before guiding them on a path most appropriate for them. It is all about listening to them, understanding their fears and desires, and helping them understand how this thing (whatever the thing is) will help them. If you find yourself in this kind of situation, use it as an opportunity to pay attention to yourself and think about how you might improve.

Author and leadership coach John Maxwell says, "Practice doesn't make perfect. Practice makes permanent." and he's right. If we are doing something often, we are cementing our habits in place, for better or worse. This is why reps do not get better, even after ten or more years of selling. They might get a little wiser about how to use their time and energy, but if they are practicing the same bad techniques, they will just keep using those same techniques. That is why intentionality is everything. Pay attention to yourself and establish measurements that will help you grow your awareness. Use practice, repetition, and visualization, but make sure the habits you are putting into practice are ones that you want to be a part of you permanently. Because eventually, they will be.

GROWTH FROM SETBACKS

Nobody hopes for setbacks in any area of life, but with the right perspective, setbacks can be a good thing. They can make us stronger, teach us how to succeed, and help us reestablish where we are in relation to where we want to be. Setbacks may be humbling in the moment, especially when they are your fault, but in the long run, they will help you build both confidence and competence. Making mistakes and experiencing setbacks is fine throughout your career, as long as you are working on learning to identify them sooner and adjust to them more quickly. If you are working on truly listening to and building a solid relationship with your customer, they will usually allow you some grace even if you do make a mistake.

Let's put an even finer point on it: if you are not making mistakes, you are probably not hitting your potential. Hockey legend Wayne Gretzky tells a story of when his father was driving him home after a loss in a youth championship hockey game. Wayne was disappointed, but his father encouraged him, telling him that none of the players on the winning team would be going on to play in the NHL. Wayne was puzzled by his dad's comment, but his dad explained that the other team's style was too structured, too conservative, too boxed-in to allow for any creativity. He was right, not a single player from the winning team went on to play in the NHL, but five kids from Wayne's team went on to play in the NHL, including Gretzky himself, the greatest hockey player ever.

You are going to make mistakes, but if you can learn and grow from them and continue putting yourself out there with courage, you will grow stronger, more confident, and more creative in your sales approach. You will become a better sales professional.

COACHES

A good coach supersedes all the other options. They hold you accountable, they have a vested interest in your growth, and they get more of your attention when coaching you on things you need to work on. The greatest athletes of all time show evidence that not only having a coach makes a difference but having the right coach is equally important. Tiger Woods won twice as many tournaments while being coached by Butch Harmon versus his other three swing coaches. Mike Tyson had a perfect record and was considered the best fighter of all time while being coached and held accountable by Cus D'Amato. The list goes on of the most elite athletes quickly ascending to the top with the right coach or tragically falling down the rankings with the lack of a good coach. I got a coach, Phil Nicaud, as I moved into my international role, and after a couple sessions, I noticed an immediate impact. Phil helped me re-balance my priorities and find purpose in serving others as I transitioned away from an individual contributor and into a player coach. As an individual who was used to winning every award and contest the company had, Phil helped me realize those awards are great but bigger things are around the corner as long as I do not care who gets the credit.

If you want to be elite at anything, it is helpful to take on the same mindset of other elite professionals, whether or not their chosen craft is the same as yours. The most important piece of that mindset is simple: never stop improving. As you read the rest of this book, keep the six areas we discussed in this chapter in mind: practicing humility, knowing your strengths and weaknesses, learning from experienced mentors, knowing your competition, practicing with intentionality, and learning from mistakes. Your mindset is everything if you want to grow.

CHAPTER 3
WHAT SELLING IS (AND WHAT IT IS NOT)

A HIGH SCHOOL FRIEND OF MINE IS ONE OF THE GREATEST direct-to-consumer salesmen I know. He would never describe himself as a salesman, and neither would his close friends. I am not describing him as one of the greatest just because he sold his solar panel company to ADT for $875 million dollars (even though he did). I am saying this because of the way he approaches sales, day in and day out. When he sells solar panels, he believes in his heart that the sale cycle is a continuous, infinite action that continues well beyond the moment when the homeowner signs their solar installation contract. He truly cares about his customers, so much that they do not even view him as a salesman.

Marc led his sales organization's culture by example. He shared with me that close to 50% of his new business comes from referrals, and the majority of those referrals are generated by the top 10% of his sales reps. I have known Marc since high school, so I can attest that his character is solid, honorable, and dependable. He delivered excellence to his customers because he stood behind his word. To him, getting this unbelievable number of referrals was always second to making sure his sales were seen through to the end and the installation was done 100% to his customers' expectations.

Marc and his team leave the customer in a better place every single time. It is not always easy. Marc told me that even when his company was at its pinnacle with locations across the US, he would step right in to help customers out in their time of need. These were usually very difficult situations, with customers expressing their difference in opinion with a good bit of emotion. Almost every time, Marc found a way to save the deal. His first step was practicing empathy while trying to fully understand the customer's expectations and how he could either meet them or collaborate on new expectations. Several of those situations ended up losing him money, but he was okay with that because he achieved his primary goal: doing right by them. Out of curiosity, I asked him if any of those deals that lost money at least yielded referrals, and he said, "I am not sure. We measure a ton of matrices, but that specific one we do not measure. When I get involved, I just want to make it right for the customer."

This mindset is what makes Marc one of the greatest salesmen I know. He is everything a salesman should be: humble, ethical, hard-working, 100% dedicated to helping his customers. His heart is in the right place, his priorities are in the right order, and his results prove that what he's doing works for his bottom line, too.

This customer-first mindset is not uncommon for CEOs and presidents. One of my past presidents, Michael Onuscheck, joined our team a month or two after we launched a medical device. I had the privilege of working booth duty with him for about three hours before someone let me know he was going to be our next president. (Yes, I might have put both feet in my mouth with my sarcastic compliments of him and his "above average" booth skills.)

We ended up working together for around eight years. Over that time I was always impressed with how he shared the vision for our company and how he would connect with us sales reps, inspiring us to make a difference in as many patients' lives as possible. Then I found out he started his career in medical devices as a sales rep himself. It all made sense now. He was able to connect with us because he understood everything we were dealing with and all the obstacles between us and helping patients (the sale). After learning of his sales past, I would occasionally ask him about selling strategies. Each time he humbly answered by letting me know he was not that good at selling, he was simply a problem solver that his customers could count on. He alluded to the fact that the customers he called on had lots of problems which gave him lots of opportunity to make things better. Constantly delivering the correct solutions to his customers made keeping him around as their sales rep, not a bad idea. It was obvious that he made problem-solving his mission, and the result was real connection and trust from customers who always had a happy emotion attached to seeing him. He was a good salesperson because the truth is, solving your customers' problems is what makes you a good salesperson, solving their core issues makes you a great salesperson, at least by my definition. This was true of Mike, even if he was too humble to admit it.

Over twenty-five years of observing nearly a thousand high-performing, customer-focused sales professionals, I have developed this definition for what selling is at its best:

Selling is connecting with your customer, understanding their needs, and articulating a genuine benefit of

the solution you are offering that will solve a real need or desire to ultimately get them to a better position than when you met them.

Let's quickly break down a few important words in this definition:

- **Connecting:** A crucial part of the sales process that is so often missed. Connecting with a customer is essential to building your understanding of them and their trust in you.
- **Understanding:** Building a true understanding of your customer will help you find the right solution and the best way to articulate how your product will benefit them in a meaningful way.
- **Articulating**: You are not forcing something on a customer. You are simply sharing, educating, or demonstrating something you believe will better their situation.
- **Genuine benefit**: No bending the truth here, you are only offering to sell your customer something that you truly believe they will benefit from.
- **Real need or desire**: You are not inventing, creating, or contributing to the reason your customer needs this product. You are responding to a real need or want in their life or work.
- **Better position**: If this product doesn't truly make their situation better, you shouldn't be trying to sell it to them.

In sales, if we do not have integrity, we do not have anything. If we are not trying to help make our customers' lives better, they will eventually figure it out and go find someone else, and rightfully so. If we are doing our jobs well, trust will build, and the relationship will grow stronger over time.

We have probably all experienced where this can go wrong. Our job is to influence, not manipulate, and the difference is simple; manipulation is when an extrinsic force is applied that results in negative outcomes, and influence is when an extrinsic force is applied that results in positive outcomes. Beware, there are some people out there who will call themselves sales professionals while looking for ways to scam or manipulate their customers. All they care about is making the sale, and if they leave the customer in a worse position than they were in before, so be it. These people give "Sales" a bad name, and they are the reason some individuals have negative stereotypes in their head when they think about sales professionals.

There are other sales approaches that, while they are ethically sound, differ from the sales approach that I am advocating for in this book. Understanding those sometimes-subtle differences is a great way to truly understand this method, why it works, and how it keeps your focus squarely on what is best for your customer.

So, in this chapter, we are going to talk briefly through a few other sales styles and how they differ from the method we will be walking through in the second half of this book. I want to be clear up front: using one of these techniques does not make you an unethical salesperson. Based on my experience and observation, I do believe that, in the real world, these other approaches will be met with increased resistance from your customers as you try to uncover their core issues. Expanding your awareness of these negative possibilities will help you be more aware of your own sales approach, making sure you do not add additional obstacles along the way.

OBJECTION HANDLING

Objection handling focuses completely on overcoming a customer's objections rather than understanding and addressing their core desire. It is like seeing that your backyard is full of standing water, a breeding ground for mosquitoes, and your solution is to just buy a can of bug spray. You are dealing with the symptom, but not the actual problem.

Objection handling is fairly common, and often if a sales rep is doing it, their heart is in the right place. If you are completely focused on crossing out a long list of objections, your sales strategy is extremely reactive or your focus is on yourself and your need to make a sale, rather than on your customer and their vision of a solution. What problem are they facing that your product could solve? What do they value most? How will your product make their situation tangibly better? If you are focused on objection handling, you will most likely miss nuggets of information, because your focus is not actually on your customer, instead focusing on their superficial objection. Here is additional food for thought: how likely are you as a consumer to give your salesperson two or three referrals after they successfully overcome five of your objections and had you sign the contract without letting you talk to your co-decision maker?

Understanding any objections your customer may have is an important part of the sales process. Rather than looking at their objections as a checklist to be completed, look at them as an opportunity to learn. Ask questions.

Give them the chance to explain why they feel the way they do. It is more important to understand where an objection is coming from than to blindly try to overcome it. Use your customer's objections as an opportunity to understand them better. Eventually, if your product is right for them, you will be able to help them envision all the positive ways it could impact their life.

HIGH-PRESSURE SALES

High-pressure sales is constantly pressuring the customer to close the sale, no matter what part of the process you are in. It generally takes place when the sales rep is more focused on serving the owner of their business than the needs of their customer. They feel pressure to complete a sale, and they transfer that pressure onto the person they are selling to. Sales reps who use this approach live by the "ABC" mantra: Always Be Closing. They ask closing questions throughout the entire sale ("We only have one left, I can hold it for you if you can commit right now and put a down payment down to show my manager you are serious"), regardless of whether the customer is ready to purchase or if the product is right for them.

This can be an effective technique at times if your only goal is to make one sale. Even if this approach does work for you, there is a good chance that your customer is committing to a purchase before they are truly ready, and that your product might not be right for them. Because you haven't taken time to listen to their needs, chances are *you* do not even know if this is the right product for them. It is not a technique that prioritizes what is best for the customer, and it is not one I advocate for.

There can be an exception to this rule, though. Say you

feel lost in a particular sale, you have been listening to the customer, but you are having a hard time gauging their interest or commitment at the moment. In this situation, a closing question can be like sending a ping from a submarine. Maybe the customer will be ready to purchase at that moment, or maybe they will not. Either way, in this situation, a closing question actually helps you to understand your customer better. You will know where they are in the process, and you have a much better idea of how to move forward.

QUESTION-BASED SELLING

A lot of selling is about asking your customer good questions so you can listen and learn from their response. Some sales approaches focus on asking questions that are more about pointing a customer's attention toward a predetermined area of pain. The aim is to prompt them to think about how negative their life would be without your product. Instead, the focus should be on building your understanding so you can eventually offer the best possible solution for their core issue (the root cause of their pain, deeper than the pain itself) and so that you can help them envision how good their life could be with your tailored solution. Question-based selling is all about probing to find a close enough pain point that needs to be addressed and helping them understand what might happen if they do not address it with your product.

I want to be clear, many reps who use this approach have their hearts in the right place. They genuinely want to help their customers. If you find yourself in a situation where a customer has actually invited you in to sell to them, this approach could be perfect. They will be more open to you jumping right in with questions to help them find the best solution for their situation. After finding important information to help them, Question-based selling can then help you motivate them to make a positive change in behavior sooner rather than later. This is a common approach for consultants who are hired by a firm to come in and tell them how to fix a problem. In these situations the consulting firm jumps right in, asking uncomfortable probing questions. Some would say the customer is expecting this form of communication because they invited the consulting firm.

That being said, I do not know about you, but I haven't been invited in on an initial sales call where the customer was totally comfortable with me asking private and personal questions. While some sales individuals may feel comfortable asking private questions anyway, I have rarely witnessed a sales rep ask personal and private questions and get truthful answers. I have observed hundreds of initial sales calls where the information received was not accurate, and it took several more interactions to build up the trust to get accurate personal information. "How much are you looking to spend?" is the most dishonestly answered question in the sales world. It is very interesting how as trust increases, honesty in answering questions like that increases as well.

Question-based selling doesn't share anything with the customer to get the conversation going. It just dives right in and starts probing from the start. In my sales process, we always share something about our product or the industry that is meaningful and interesting to the customer to start the conversation, something that will initiate conversation and give you a chance to listen and learn from them.

It is not my goal to be overly negative about question-based selling. Like I said, it can be great in the right situations. However, its focus on negative emotions during every sales interaction will not make a customer feel good about you, and even if you convince them they have a need, they may choose to go with a different business to meet that need. A close friend of mine owns a Christian Brothers mechanic shop, and he regularly has clients come to him after speaking to another shop that pointed out some needed repairs in such a negative way that the customer didn't want to work with them. So, the negative question-based approach technically worked to influence the potential customer to get the much-needed repairs done, just not at their shop.

This just emphasizes two of the core pillars of my sales process: focusing on positive emotion more than negative, and understanding your customer. If you can do those two things, you will still be able to help your customer understand how your product can make their life better, but you will do so in a way that will make them feel good about you and your connection over the long haul and help them feel comfortable referring you to a friend.

TRANSACTIONAL SELLING

In transactional selling, the focus is solely on one individual transaction with a customer. There is nothing wrong with this from an ethical standpoint, but if this is your approach, you are thinking too small, and your focus is in the wrong place. A sale should be more than just a sale. The majority of your focus should not be on the product, or on the transaction itself. Instead, it should be on your customer, on forming a connection with them, and on inviting them to come on a journey with you that will last long beyond this one transaction.

In transactional selling, often a sale will occur whether you do everything perfect as the sales rep or not. You are just there to see the sale through and make sure there are no mistakes that could prevent the sale or cause a chargeback. Some industries even refer to the sales rep involved in transactional selling as a "high-paid order taker."

If you find yourself in a position like this, in a job where you can survive by taking orders because it is obvious and well-known that your product is superior, then let me challenge you and encourage you to break the mold. You could be doing so much more than transactional selling. You have the potential to push your limits, crush your quotas, double your sales.

Millions of dollars have been spent on fast food "point of sale" studies. Several well-designed studies proved that "point of sale" revenue can be increased by over 25% if something is blindly offered before the order is taken at the intercom. This is why today, when you pull up to the fast food intercom, you are greeted by a voice offering a menu item that you were not thinking of. This is also why they follow up your order with "Do you want to supersize that?" or "What else would you like?" When I worked at McDonald's, I was the self-proclaimed 15-year-old apple pie-selling champion. My pitch was simple: "We just had a batch of hot apple pies come out. You want me to grab you two? They are only 69 cents."

Even in fast food, the very definition of transactional selling, it is always possible to do more. So how much more must this be true in other industries, where you actually have an opportunity to develop a long-term connection with your customer?

If you are stuck in transactional selling, find a way to break free. Start by offering something they might not have been thinking about. Learn from their response. If they're a repeat customer, happy with your service, see if you can get a referral, a social media post, or an online review from them. There is always room to think bigger, and for anyone stuck in a loop of transactional selling, there is always room to grow.

PRODUCT EXPERTS

A product expert knows their product better than anyone else. They can tell you why it is great, how to use it, and how some features are better than the competition's. However, your job as a sales rep is not to explain to a customer how your product's features are better. Your job is to translate those details into real information and help the customer see how your product could make *their* life better.

Product experts know their products, but sales reps know their customers. I have witnessed many companies across different industries recruit new sales reps with this exact philosophy in mind. In some cases, if a particular sales rep has a strong relationship with a client and a new company in the industry wants to work with this high-profile client, then the company will hire this rep without worrying about their level of product knowledge. Most companies have built-in infrastructures to support their new hires, allowing sales managers to put more emphasis on hiring reps with relationships or ones who know how to connect with people.

Companies want to believe that all their top sales reps are product experts. On the contrary, these companies are slightly mistaken. These top reps may be above average in product knowledge, but where they test off the charts is in awareness, empathy, and trustworthiness, which leads to really knowing the customer. Now let us talk about the rest of the sales team and exclude the top reps. Let's imagine I'm selling a product that I'm extremely knowledgeable about, but I don't know much about the customer and I am having a difficult time getting them to share any pertinent information. In this scenario I will not be able to articulate how this product could impact them directly, I will not be able to share the benefits of the product, or the reason they should buy it. Now imagine I know a great deal about the customer. In this scenario, I can paint a very realistic picture for them, one full of positive emotions where their situation will greatly improve with this product and in a way that is specifically meaningful to them. Now that is powerful.

I once sold to a doctor who placed a high value on efficiency. His philosophy was that if he could be very efficient with his time, then he could possibly help one or two more patients that day instead of forcing them to wait for another opening in his schedule. He would ultimately be helping more patients, and helping as many patients as possible was his goal. I knew him well enough to understand how important time management was to him, and these details influenced my approach with him in two ways.

First, it really helped me qualify if my product was the right fit for him in the first place. For instance, if my device happened to be less expensive but it slowed him down in surgery, then trying to convince him it was the right product for his budget wouldn't be a good use of his time (or mine).

Second, if I am confident and know my device will save him time in surgery, then I know without a doubt it is what he needs. Now moving forward in the sales cycle I will have confidence and proceed knowing exactly how to present it to him. "Hey Doc, if you decide to use this product, you will be done with your cases in half the time. Imagine yourself in the hall between procedures waiting for the nurses to flip rooms because you are done in a fraction of the time. Your schedule will flow perfectly, your patients will love you, and you will be able to squeeze in two or three more procedures a day." This helped him to see that I cared about his priorities, that I understood him, and that if he selected to use this superior product, he would be making a positive impact toward his core desire.

Knowing your product is great, but there is nothing more important than knowing your customer. If your focus is on knowing them, you will build trust, you will understand what matters most to them, and you will know how to help them envision a world where the product you are selling makes them the hero.

FIELD MARKETING

Marketing and sales have a few things in common. At their core, both of them are a fight for two things: attention and retention. Both are an effort to help a customer to learn about a product, care about a product, and remember a product. Once in a while, a company with an existing sales force will hire a marketing company to help them launch a new product or kick off a new marketing campaign, and this usually results in the sales force being encouraged to memorize a very specific message to ensure that there is only one consistent voice in the field. The reps' creativity and originality is removed in favor of consistency in the marketing. The rep's ability to tailor a message to best fit the needs of each individual customer is also taken away.

Downstream marketing is, by definition, the research of potential clients followed by the creation of a broad message that resonates with the largest percentage of the target audience as possible. While there is value in creating a consistent, branded message, it works best when it works hand-in-hand with a sales force that can customize the message to the specific needs of individual customers. Marketing is all about intentionality and consistent messaging, but without authentic connection with the customer. While intentional messaging is obviously a huge part of sales, the delivery of that message needs to be able to vary by customer. The message is not a standard one-size-fits-all, because connection is at the foundation of sales. Authentic connection needs to be tailored for each individual customer along with being adjusted for the specific situation each customer is dealing with.

Here's the tricky part, even without their company forcing them to, lots of sales reps become marketers without even realizing it. They develop in their own style a smooth sales pitch that feels good to them and seems to be efficient. They perceive it to be efficient because it explains all the advantages and resonates with a decent amount of their prospects. They have accidentally created their own marketing campaign. This happens for a couple reasons: reps getting a little too confident or trying to be too efficient. Either way, they are not taking the time to listen to their customer, understand their specific needs, and identify the core issue. All of which are needed to help customers see how this product would uniquely benefit them. Here is an easy test to use on yourself: if you have a go-to sales pitch that could be recorded and played back as a commercial, then what you are doing is probably marketing.

This matters for a few reasons. For one, it can backfire

completely. If I had given my time-sensitive doctor a pitch centered around how this product may add a bit more time to each case but was much more ergonomic and comfortable for the doctor to use or how studies show my product will last 12 years versus the 10 years other products last, he would have stopped listening and probably never taken me seriously again. Pitching someone on a benefit without understanding whether it will actually benefit them, is the same thing as throwing a dart blindfolded. You might hit a few random numbers, but you are more likely to miss the whole board and upset Chad, the guy who has to repair the drywall.

Even when using a "Field Marketing" approach feels like it works on a customer, it is not a sustainable approach for your future one-on-one sales calls with them. It could result in a transaction, but it doesn't help you build a relationship with your customer or understand anything about their needs. You are ending in basically the same place you started, and if you have something else to share with them, they may listen, but there will not be a deep level of trust or connection built. In general, reps who take this approach have a much harder time getting referrals, especially early on. Now reps who show genuine humility and an interest in understanding the customer can get a referral even on the very first interaction.

Marketing, with its emphasis on messaging, still plays a pivotal role. A robust marketing department in a sales organization can make a great impact on revenue by equipping sales reps with adaptable content allowing reps to tailor the message to each customer's unique needs. However, while marketing leans on messaging, the heart of Authentic SALES lies on connection.

While various strategies discussed in this chapter hold

value in their respective contexts, I'm confident that sales professionals eager to embrace Authentic SALES will find it easier to implement, encounter fewer obstacles, and derive greater pleasure from applying it.

As we move through the remaining pages of this book, we'll dive deep into my distinct sales process, understanding the powerful nuances that can transform your results. Together, we'll pinpoint those subtle changes that will mold you into the most authentic and effective sales professional you can be.

CHAPTER 4
CONNECTION AND THE JOURNEY

AROUND THE YEAR 2005, I MADE MORE TRIPS TO THE SPRINT Mobile store than I can count or care to admit. All these visits were in an attempt to find a cell phone that would actually do what I needed it to do. As a sales rep, my phone was my life. I had to be available to communicate with customers anytime they wanted to reach me. Which sometimes was very difficult, due to the poor quality phones that were coming out around that time, lack of technology in the cell towers, and the spotty reception that Sprint offered across the rural parts of my territory. I was consistently frustrated with my phone. Poor battery life, inconsistent functionality, weak signal, slow processing, everything you *didn't* want in a cell phone became typical for me.

To make matters worse, every time I went into the Sprint store to try to find a solution, the reps I encountered would make me feel like I was the only one having these problems, implying that maybe I was the one doing something wrong. Then, before even handling the problem at hand, they would try to upsell me on accessories for the phone I was having problems with. A few times they suggested trying out a different model phone, but those all failed, too. The product Sprint was offering me was not working, and the sales reps I worked with were just making things worse.

Then, during one of these frustrating visits, a sales rep named Katrina stepped in to take over and try to fix the problem. She was the first rep in this store who actually listened to me with awareness and empathy. She took the time to understand my world and my issues, and she dug in until she had uncovered the root of the problem. She easily could have just given me what I was asking for, an older reliable model, but instead, she used her awareness of my situation combined with her expertise as a sales rep to lead me to a solution that actually solved my problem. For those of you who are interested in the solution, a cell phone with the longest battery life and a more expensive cellular plan with unlimited roaming.

From that day forward, every time I went into that Sprint store, I'd request to work with Katrina. If she was with another customer, I would wait for her, even if other reps were free. I knew that she was competent, and that she would take the time to listen to me and understand what I wanted, without trying to sell me something I didn't need. Years of buying accessories and upgrading phones, returning to the same store and requesting her, I suggested to her that she should get into Medical sales or Pharma. She eventually did, and now, nearly 10 years later, Katrina is a multiple-time President Club recipient for a Pharmaceutical company.

Let's revisit a fundamental truth about sales that we introduced in the first chapter: you buy from who you like. Why? Because, ultimately, sales is not about closing questions, or giving a huge discount, or a superficial conversation. It is about creating a genuine connection that will build trust with your customer.

When I walked out of that Sprint store, Katrina and I did not become hang-out buddies, but she had earned my complete trust. I would most likely buy whatever she suggested during any visit, because I felt that she understood what I needed. Even if she tried to upsell me, I wouldn't second guess her motives. This is what you should strive for with all of your customers. That every time you finish a call with them, they will look forward to the next time they get to work with you. That they share your name with a friend in the market of the product you sell.

There are a million different reasons a customer might like you. Maybe they trust you, or admire you, or enjoy being around you. Maybe they feel a little bit sorry for you. Maybe they appreciate you for saving them money, or for teaching them something, or for making their family or coworkers happy. Maybe your presence makes them feel like they are in charge, and they enjoy that feeling. Maybe over time, you have formed a real friendship with them.

When I started at Edward Jones Financial as a financial advisor, I knocked on over two thousand residential doors seeking new customers. As great as the training is with Edward Jones, it is still extremely hard to connect with people as an uninvited solicitor on their doorstep. While I ultimately became close with several customers and their families, there is one older couple that stands out in my memory.

The wife was as sweet as could be, but the husband was difficult for me to read. When I first met them, the wife answered the door and allowed me to talk about my new job and my goal of opening a new Edward Jones office on the east side of town. As we were conversing, her husband came to the door to rescue her from me and stop our conversation. He was very confident but polite. Instead of rudely sending me on my way, like 50% of all my prospects did, he wanted to shut me down with wit.

He asked what I was doing, and then he shared some of his very strong objections. For example, he shared that in his retirement, he day traded and did very well. So, why would he need a financial advisor? He asked about my fees, which were higher than the online broker service he was using. He laughed at the educational seminars that I host monthly in town. He explained his years of experience, even with foreign markets, and told me he didn't need any more education on it.

Whereas his wife was more open. She expressed that while she didn't have the experience her husband had, she was interested in learning. So, I offered to come back with some of my educational materials to do private lessons. She was excited about the idea, but he was not, and he showed it.

The first time I came back for his wife's investment lesson, I gave him research on two stocks, in two different industries. He didn't like either one, and he told me why. On my next visit, equipped with this new information of his dislikes, I was able to bring him research on something similar to what he trades. He acted unimpressed, but this time, he read it, and when leaving, he told me why the analysts were wrong. He was finally doing more than just trying to debate me, he was engaging with me and taking in the information I was sharing with him.

I had six scheduled lessons with his wife, and that gave me several opportunities to understand him. So, you'd better believe that every time I showed up, I brought him research that was closer and closer to what he traded. Finally, when I started sharing research that received his seal of approval, he came and sat with us. His wife started investing with me, and I would hand-deliver trade confirmations to her and also bring more research for him. Eventually, he started asking me about his investments that were not a part of his day-trading portfolio, his mutual funds. I had finally won him over because I didn't waste his time. He liked my approach of dropping off research instead of trying to sell to him or even worse debate him. He had fun with it, and as I got closer to the target, it got more interesting to him. It took time, but it built our connection, and eventually it led to a working relationship that was valuable and genuine for both of us.

In more than three decades of experience, one of the most vital things I have learned is that sales is all about connection. While that connection can take different forms, it can have a huge impact as long as it is authentic. If you connect with your customers sincerely, learn about what is important to them, and bring authentic value to their lives, you will be well on your way to where you want to be.

MADE FOR CONNECTION

We were made for connection with others. We crave it when we do not have it, and it makes us feel more complete when we do have it.

We want to connect to people. We want to be around people who "get" us, who hear us and understand us on a wavelength that a lot of people do not. Like a quarterback and a wide receiver who seem to read each other's minds, or like two strangers who run up on a car accident and start helping in unison without having to say a word. This is the kind of connection we want to create with our customers, something genuine and truly meaningful.

A running joke in our family is everyone hides or acts busy when I need someone to hold a flashlight for any task I'm doing in the dark, like working on a car at night, wiring a generator to the house during a hurricane, or working on an air conditioner in the hot attic. I totally get it. I'm a jerk when the light is shined everywhere but where I need it. This simple task becomes an extremely stressful and unpaid job. The fact is I haven't spent enough time explaining what I am trying to accomplish to my three sons in these situations. I am expecting them to just know what I am thinking. If I were to put in the effort to build up that level of connection with them on these projects, maybe eventually they would volunteer instead of physically leaving the room when asked. Please keep in mind, in this situation I am the customer and my sons represent the sales rep.

It is extremely rare to have a customer hand you a playbook with step-by-step instructions on how to sell to them. This burden lies solely on you as the sales rep to figure it out, and the faster you do so the stronger the connection (and sale). Florian, a successful pacemaker rep in Germany that I have spent a lot of time with, shared with me that he is the son of a tradesman. He worked with his father when he was young, and to keep his dad from saying unflattering words toward him, Florian learned to anticipate what his dad would need next. It became a challenge and a game to him. This now translates perfectly to working with fast-moving surgeons in the operating room, staying one step ahead of them and ultimately connecting with the surgeon on a level that means the most to them in that situation. For Florian this mentality led to a very successful cardiac implant career. As you can imagine having a competent "stay one step ahead" strategy during heart surgery is extremely valuable to a cardiac surgeon. Today, Florian is over the entire country of Germany managing a very strong and competent team.

This can play out differently with different customers. Not everyone is looking for a new best friend. However, that doesn't mean you can't connect with them authentically on a deep professional level and form a bond that will be extremely meaningful to both of you. Every customer is looking for someone who can connect with what matters to them, the problems they are facing, the things they value, and how their situation could improve in a meaningful way.

I saw this play out with a surgeon I sold to who was a bit of an unusual guy. People told me he was not easy to figure out, and that he rarely allowed reps in the operating room with him, which is highly unusual. I knew he was a private person who worked with a high volume of patients. Other than that I didn't have much to go on, especially to connect with him on.

For over a year, I tried to get his business through lunches and nice presentations in his office. It was hard for me to find interesting and meaningful Reasons to Return, so it would often take months for me to get in to see him again, and when I did return, he would ask why I was back. It was clear that he was not impressed with what I was doing or my product.

So, I emotionally gave up on trying to impress him. I went into my next meeting with him, with an "I do not care" attitude. I started the meeting by listing out all the negative aspects of what I was sharing, anything he might find an objection with. No small talk, I jumped right in and was straightforward, sharing contraindications and surgical complications first then followed it up with my best guess of a benefit for him and his patients. I didn't bother trying to impress him or build up the product as the next best thing (which it happened to be). I just said what I had to say. One way to sum it up, this was definitely the "under-promise" portion to the saying, "under promise and over deliver."

Well, I didn't know it at the time, but that approach was what finally cracked open the door for me. I found out later that trying to sell him would get you negative points. However, when I focused on sharing my product knowledge with a straightforward approach without small talk or marketing terms, I started connecting with him. I didn't fully realize it at the time, but I was finally starting to connect with him on what he valued most.

I did two things that ultimately won this doctor over when he finally agreed to do a case with my product. First, I took it upon myself to find and teach the circulating RN and X-ray tech to help them understand what we were doing. Then, I went to talk to the patient, educate them, answer their questions, and ultimately calm their nerves about the procedure. When the doctor saw me interact with his patient before the procedure, we really started to connect. He valued experience in his reps and outcomes for his patients more than anything else, and he started to see that I valued that, too. As I observed him with his patients, I started to understand that while he might have come across as a little bit odd to sales reps, he was amazing with his patients.

During our second surgery together, I handed off my product and attempted to exit the operating room, which is what he wanted reps to do. But this time he told me he wanted me to stay in the operating room with him.

Everyone was surprised and confused, including his staff. I waited intensely to see if I had done something he did not approve of, instead I was taken aback when he started asking about other uses for our product and the outcomes I honestly saw. Apparently, my interaction with his patients and his operating staff had a bigger impact on him than I would have imagined.

Sometimes connection is easy, but sometimes our customers can surprise us by not responding to even our most genuine attempts at connection in the way we would expect. That is why it is so important to always be working to understand your customer better. Take a moment to see how they want to receive what you are sharing. If you really know your stuff (which you should), you should be able to stay ahead of what they might expect and let them know they can count on you.

It is natural to want your customer to like you. This is actually a good thing—it means you care. Just be aware that a decent amount of your customers will only value a professional connection. For the small business owners or high-level professionals, this connection might be more important to them. Do not try beating a square peg through a round hole trying to connect in a way they do not find valuable. Knowing their favorite football team is fine, but it doesn't add value. Instead, learning more about how they got into their industry. Or what their biggest values are in their work? Or what experiences in their career helped shape their outlook on what they do? Now we are getting somewhere. They will most likely enjoy talking about that, instead of personal stuff. Also, you will learn more useful information about them. Just to be clear, never lead a sales call with this. These are things for you to implement when you're finished sharing what needs to be shared.

Picture yourself at a wedding reception with friends. You are trying to tell a story, and no one seems to understand the point you are trying to make. Then, just like a scene in a sitcom, someone you do not know walks over from across the room, greets a couple of your friends, and starts listening to your story. You find yourself repeating parts because your close friends are not getting it, but the person you do not know understands exactly what you are saying, and even helps explain it to everyone else. You do not know this person, but you have an immediate connection with them. You might even say out loud, "This guy gets me." That is the kind of connection you want to form with your customers. You want them to feel understood. When you are not around you want them to tell others to do business with you because "you get it".

Your customers live in the real world, they understand that you have a job to do. They know that ultimately, one of your goals as a sales rep is to earn their business. So in most cases, they will actually appreciate it if you focus on bringing them true value within that role. Most customers will be able to sniff out inauthentic questions or insincere motives. They can see it when you are just trying to butter them up to make a sale. If you focus on connecting through what matters to them most, you can earn their trust. They will start to feel like you "get" them, and they will see that you truly want to help.

AUTHENTIC CONNECTION

I witnessed one of the most well-intentioned sales reps crash and burn trying to connect superficially. I traveled to Mississippi with a fellow sales rep to meet with a purchasing director. My colleague was an experienced sales professional with many years under his belt, an excellent grasp of pricing, and a huge heart. He was a little bit old-school, but it seemed to work just fine because all in all, he came across like a caring sales rep. When he would meet a customer in their office, one of his favorite moves to break the ice was to look around the room and find something that he could personally connect with. In this case, a picture of a sailboat caught his eye right away. My colleague had boating experience, and he thought if they could connect on that point, it might start off our meeting on a more pleasant tone. We were anticipating a non-enjoyable pricing discussion.

So, my colleague pointed to the picture on the wall and said, "Oh, you are into sailing?" The purchasing director looked him in the eye and said, "No," then paused for an uncomfortable three seconds and followed it up with, "I just put that picture up to see how many sales reps mention it."

My colleague's motives were pure, and his heart was in the right place. Failing to connect made his genuine attempt feel inauthentic, because he knew that ultimately, we were there to sell him something. I would suggest waiting to the end of the meeting before attempting this kind of common-ground connection. Get the business out of the way first then try and find common ground to connect on if you want. You will find doing it in this order will increase your chances of it feeling authentic to your customer. Keep in mind, if you bring an immense amount of value on the business side, you won't need to connect on a personal level.

Ultimately, my colleague and I were able to hone in on what this customer really cared about. We were able to listen and understand what really mattered to him, which was ultimately price and budgeting for future expenses. He wanted a guarantee that we would not raise our prices for the next fiscal year and we would not sneak in new products that were not in our catalog. This led to a meaningful conversation about how we could honor him and help him hit his budget next year. That shift happened when we directed our focus toward what mattered most to him. By staying away from a discussion about patient outcomes or the advantages of our devices, we showed him that his priorities mattered to us and it ultimately allowed us to form a connection with him, even after a rocky start.

Not every interaction is going to be perfect. In some cases, it is going to take some work to convince your customers that you are genuine, that you really do care about them, their values, and their problems. Make it your mindset to understand your customer first, then connect on common ground or what is most meaningful to them. This doesn't mean you have to be perfect, and it is okay to fail. Just make sure you learn from each failure. Approaching your customers with authenticity will lead you to success in your career, and it will lead you to truly helping your customers in the ways that matter most to them.

This is not just true with customers. If you want your company to stand the test of time, it is crucial that connection is built into everything you do, including with your own co-workers or employees. A great example of this is the MLM (multi-level marketing) sales model, where everyone who joins a company is encouraged to bring on people to sell under them and incentivized by receiving commission on everything those people sell (as well as their own sales). Many of these companies do not last, because people just jump in for the money. The companies that fail in MLM view the new recruits as numbers or dollars. They only care about the people under them selling because their paycheck will get bigger if they do well.

The MLM companies that survive and do well are the ones that have connection imprinted on their DNA. Their people truly care about others in the organization. If they bring someone on to sell under them, they will put in the time and work to truly invest in helping them succeed. People aren't just in it for themselves, they are in it for each other. When that level of authentic caring is built into your company's culture, you will have a real chance to thrive, no matter what your business model is.

A close friend of mine sold a commercial cleaning service. I would listen to his conversations with customers. It was so obvious that he cared about his clients and making sure their offices were clean and the waste baskets were empty on the days he promised. Every one of his clients believed he cared, and they would all help him with referrals or as references. His problem was that this business was not scalable because of staffing, all the cleanings took place during a night shift. When Trey and his wife found a multi-level marketing company that aligned with their core values, they were off to the races. Because of their customer-centric approach, it was extremely easy for Trey and Leslie to have an immediate impact changing people's lives, literally. They are now coaching thousands and thousands of people on health, weight loss, and overall well-being. The take-away for this story—do not stop caring about those you serve. If it does not pay off in this career, continue to make it a part of who you are and it will eventually pay off big time. Meanwhile, you will be making the culture around you attractive.

If you want to preserve or improve your company's culture, it starts by making sure you are recruiting the right people into your company, people who will prioritize connection in everything they do. I believe job interviews for sales positions are often conducted in a counterproductive manner. The standardized questions that are usually asked can show you if a person is a polished speaker and good at preparing for an interview. They do not show you anything about whether the interviewee has the ability to connect with people, and they do not truly give you the chance to connect with them, either.

When it comes to connecting with potential future employees, one of my former VP of Sales, Allen, was one of the best I have ever seen. When he went into an interview, his number one priority was building a connection with the interviewee or allowing them the opportunity to connect with him. He had tough questions to ask, but he would save those for later, after he connected with them or got a feel for their ability to connect with him. He understood the value of connection, both as a skill for any potential sales reps to possess and as a way for him to sell the interviewee on joining the company.

In 2012, Allen's authentic interviewing style allowed him to recruit one of the best sales reps in the medical device industry, Brad. This guy was no joke, he had won Rep of the Year four times at three different companies. You would think to convince a guy like Brad to leave his company for yours, you'd have to offer him a lot of money or something else to sweeten the deal, but that was not the case here. Allen focused on building a connection with him, and in the end, Allen brought Brad on board to work for us just like any of our other reps, standard salary and commission structure, no special privileges.

It was all about the connection they formed, and the common ground Allen found with him. Brad was a male

RN, and he cared deeply about his patient's outcomes as much as the physicians he worked with, which was also one of Allen's core values. Brad was also very competitive. Just before he was formally offered the job, he asked Allen, "Who's your best rep? I want to meet the guy I am going to beat." Three weeks later, Brad was in my house, sitting at my dining room table, eating dinner with my family. Just like that, a lifelong friendship was born, and I had another skilled rep to compete with.

THE JOURNEY

One of my son's signature phrases when he was little was "Let's do it together." "Hey Dad, let's build a car ramp together." "Hey Dad, let's do a puzzle together." Every time he said it, it was like a tractor beam pointed straight to my heart. He got an immediate response from me every time, I would stop what I was doing and play.

The concept of doing something *together* is meaningful, and it is another reason why authentic connection is so important in sales. Helping a customer see how a product could impact them is a mini journey, one that requires investment from you. Now, if you have formed a genuine connection based on the improvement of their situation and you invite them to go on a journey with you, it can be extremely powerful. A quick example of this is if you are on the cuff of winning a big award or mile marker achievement and you reach out to your loyal customers to help with referrals or purchases, then you are inviting them in on a journey. Believe it or not, people enjoy being a part of a winning team or huge accomplishment. This is the premise behind every sponsorship, from little league baseball to local fun runs to World Cup soccer tournament. Keep in mind you will need to approach this differently from industry to industry and even from customer to customer.

I want to preface this next story, this is not an example for you to emulate. The reason I want to share it is to demonstrate just how wide of a spectrum there is in terms of taking your customers on a journey. This particular "journey" takes place in two different directions, the sales rep's journey with the customer joining in on the action and the flip side of this is observing a customer's journey where you join in on the excitement.

Stephen is an auto sales professional who I greatly admire. Over the past 25+ years, he has worked at a few different dealerships, at each dealership he was able to break the franchise record of selling the most cars in a given month. Stephen is a sales guy through and through, and his management style is similar. For the majority of his career, he worked for one dealer who owned four different dealerships in a fairly small town. The dealerships were next to each other, and the sales individuals could sell from any of the lots. Because Stephen led by example and was a natural when it came to developing sales reps, the Owners would staff his Honda dealership with mostly new hires.

About five years back, Stephen and his young team were doing a great job increasing sales. Mostly due to their growth mindset, and writing their goals down for everyone to see. Three months in a row they were able to beat the previous month's sales. They were about to celebrate back-to-back best years ever. The team's morale at this Honda store was was flying high. The only problem---they were heading into December, typically the worst month in the car industry. Stephen wanted to keep the positive momentum rolling and the team's excitement high by demonstrating how an interesting stretch goal and hard work would beat any slow month. They had some extra motivation from a fellow coworker who had recently passed away. They were driven by dedicating $100 per car to the hospital that was treating Brad during his illness.

So, Stephen did what Stephen does best and made an audacious wager: he was going to set up a tent in the woods behind the dealership and call it home until his team broke the record of "Most cars sold in a month." Not just for December, but the best sales month the dealership ever had in its twenty-five-year history. I talked to him the day he made this wager and laughed because, besides it being the worst month possible for car sales, there was snow on the ground in Ohio.

Day one, Stephen jumped right in and led by example, emulating a successful sales rep getting on the phone and drumming up some business. He opened up his contact list and started smiling and dialing the customers he had acquired and taken care of over the past nineteen years. These customers were loyal, a staggering 75% of them were repeat buyers. Stephen had a genuine connection with these customers. Over the years they have all been on some sort of journey with Stephen because he was always up to something outside the box, and now they were about to be asked to join him on another journey.

Stephen started telling these past customers about this crazy bet he had made with his sales team, and they laughed because they knew Stephen and they knew he was telling the truth about living in a tent down behind the Honda store. Stephen started off by asking them to help him by sending a referral or making a social media post. What he did not fully realize was that he was inviting them along on his crazy journey. In one way or another, most of them joined him on this journey. Some of them came to the dealership and bought a car. One customer even bought two cars and made Stephen personally deliver it during her Christmas party and present it as a gift to her daughter. Several other past customers who didn't buy referred friends to the dealership. The rest of his past customers joined in by sharing his social media posts. They engaged with his mission, and suddenly Stephen had an army of supporters journeying along with him.

Stephen stayed in that tent day after day, week after week. The sales team even took turns visiting Stephen and his campfire after hours. Some of them even spent a night camping out in the woods with him. His sales reps were all in. They may not have had any longtime customers to call, but they were calling and making sure their recent customers were happy and if they would, share some of the camping posts or even better send a referral. Before the month was even over, it was obvious that the young sales individuals at the Honda store were going to have larger commission checks than the veterans across the street. The fun they were having was contagious. Sales reps from the other three stores wanted in on the fun and sold a few new Hondas also.

Here's the interesting part, vendors wanted to get involved. As the excitement started to spread, their lenders, warranty companies, insurance companies, and the mobile detailer they used, wanted in on the action. They saw the increased volume and excitement on social media and wanted to share in both. These vendors joining in on Stephen's journey won them credit with him. It deepened each of their relationships with him and helped them hit their monthly numbers.

All this excitement and silliness did not help with customers who randomly stopped in to buy a car. These brand-new customers could care less about Stephen sleeping in a tent behind the dealership because they had no connection with him. That being said, for those new customers who did choose to buy from his dealership in December, Stephen would introduce himself afterward, thank them for helping get him out of the tent, take a picture with them and their new car, and ask them if he can tag them in the post. So in a way, they were a part of the best sales month this dealership has ever had in 25 years.

Stephen's campout re-engaged prior customers and, ultimately, engaged some new ones with what we can all agree was a pretty silly journey. They had come together to be part of the greatest sales month this small rural Honda Store in Ohio had ever seen.

Obviously, not every "End of the Year" sale is going to look like this. I am definitely not advocating to pitch a tent every time you have a slow month. I would like to emphasize the power and engagement of a journey. This goes both ways—you inviting customers to be a part of your journey or you joining them on their journey. Examples of this are a store about to serve their one millionth customer, a Go Fund Me account for local tragedy, sponsoring an underprivileged youth program, bringing awareness to Cribs for Kids, a golf tournament for kids without dads, or a walk for PD awareness. If you truly care for your customers, they can become some of your best advocates. The connection you form during a journey will last far beyond any normal sales experience and definitely yield more referrals.

SHARE YOUR STORY

It may feel strange practicing how to talk about yourself. Nonetheless, learning how to share your story, especially the parts of your story that are most significant to your customer, is a very important trust-building skill you can develop as a sales rep. If you can do this well, followed by behaving in a predictable, reliable way, you will build credibility and trust with them over time.

This is where learning the right way to share your backstory comes in. What is your personal connection to the work you do? Why do you care? Why are you selling this particular product when you could be selling something else, or not working in sales at all? What can you share about yourself that will help your customer understand that you are doing this for bigger reasons than just the money? What is your "tagline" that a customer can share with a friend after they've had a great experience with you? How can you make it as easy as possible for them to both understand who you are and refer you to others in the future?

This will look different for everyone, and for every industry. What you sell is important and if you truly care about the work you are doing, you should be able to find a meaningful personal backstory to share with your customer, no matter what you are selling.

It could be incredibly personal, like what I shared with people when I sold security systems: "I walked in on my house being burglarized when I was ten years old. I sell security systems now because I do not want any kid to have to go through what I did."

Or, it could be more general, but still authentic: "I got into auto sales because I am a gearhead and love cars. Now that I have been selling them for a few years I realize how much joy the right car brings to people and the joy all the new features bring to their kids." As long as it is authentic to you and meaningful to your customer, it will help build trust and allow you to start connecting.

In practice, it helps to think of this as a tagline split into two sentences. The first sentence is your backstory—where you have been, and what motivated you to do what you are doing today. The second sentence is your new story—how you are hoping to help other people through the work you do. With a little bit of forethought, you can give your customer a powerful snapshot of who you are very quickly.

Here are a couple of examples of what this could look like:

- Backstory: "When my dad passed away, he didn't have life insurance and it crippled our family financially." New story: "I want to be the guy who prevents that from happening to other families."
- Backstory: "I grew up with a single mom and a car that barely ran." New story: "I wanted to be like the owner of the repair shop who always helped us, even when my mom could not pay."
- Backstory: "My accounts got hacked into, and it was scary, stressful, an overall mess for me, and I lost a lot of money." New story: "I sell this software now because I do not want another small business owner to ever have to deal with that."

Take a moment to think about it right now. Who are you? What is your bigger "why" that motivates you to do what you do? What positive impact do you want to make in your customers' lives? Jot down some notes. Make a list of ideas.

Think about how to summarize your backstory and your new story in one sentence each. This can be a powerful tool for you to use as you work to build a connection with your customer and help them get to know the most important parts of you.

IT IS NOT ABOUT YOU

Stop me if you have heard this before: the single most important thing about sales is that it is all about your customer. It is not about you, it is not about your product, it is not about your company, it is about them. It is about making their experience with you the best it can be and making their situation better with the product you are selling.

You can't fake this. Your heart needs to be in it, and your motives need to be pure all the way through. You need to be the kind of sales rep you'd want to send your elderly relative to. If your heart is genuine, your customer will feel it. If you're in it for their money, they will feel that, too.

If your motives are truly pure, you can create a connection built on trust that will last. You will have more empathy for your customer and their needs, find common ground to help you connect, and engage with them in a way that feels like you are being yourself. Not only will it build trust on their end, but it will also feel much more authentic, energizing, and sustainable on your end.

We are not far from artificial intelligence being able to perform most parts of the sales process better than sales reps. We might be there already. One thing that A.I. will have a hard time duplicating—authentic human connection. It is also what separates you from other sales reps, and it is what separates you from a mindless computer that can list out all the advantages of a product it wants you to buy.

It is impossible for artificial intelligence to truly care about the person it is selling to because they do not have empathy for them or their situation. This is where you can really make a difference.

If your heart is in the right place, your actions will follow. I was once working on selling to a doctor in the Middle East. With most of my sales calls in other countries, I am there to assist the local rep, so I want to make sure I earn their trust and demonstrate my sales process to them firsthand. Most of our sales calls are in person and some via video conference call. I had been working with the local reps there for a while. They had a new surgeon that they were calling on for a while and were hoping I could help influence him to finally commit and start implanting our device. We had this call scheduled for two weeks because the surgeon was very busy, and just as I was getting ready to meet them online in the morning, Hurricane Ida hit.

Our yard flooded, and we lost power in my house for ten days. Despite the Hurricane making a direct hit, I felt that if I told the reps that I could not make our scheduled sales call because I didn't have power, they might see it as me just making an excuse. So, I popped out my electric meter and used a small generator to backfeed my house. I flipped off all the breakers except for my office and one other room. That gave me just enough power for my computer, my internet router, and a fan for the rest of my family. I was able to jump on the call with them. While the fact that I didn't have power never came up until the end of our conversation—I still wanted to keep the focus on them and what I had prepared for the physician—when they found out what I had done to make the call happen, their reaction was way stronger than I expected. (I hate to say it, but after you have survived twenty-plus hurricanes, you sort of get used to it.)

I was honored when both the physician and the local reps recognized and mentioned how committed I was to them, it is safe to say trust was built. For me, it was nothing more than seeing through a commitment. I truly cared about helping these reps, and I knew the only way I was going to get closer to them was to do what I said I was going to do. Also, I coached several reps in the Middle East, and I wanted them to observe me using my own sales process that I had been sharing with them. I needed to be on that call to prove to them that this sales process works across all continents and cultures.

The more you focus on forming authentic, meaningful connections with your customers based on their needs and values, the more they will believe that you have their back. That you care about them. And that you are in it to give them an advantage in their own journey, not to take advantage of them. You will build trust, loyalty, and long-term stability in your relationship with them, and they will feel much more at ease going (and staying) on this journey with you.

CHAPTER 5
AWARENESS QUOTIENT

In 1984, Steve Jobs introduced the first Macintosh computer. This level of processing power available to people in their own homes was revolutionary, and among its many new features was the ability to speak. The computer's text-to-speech capability was a major part of Jobs' initial presentation when he introduced the computer to the world. It could say whatever you wanted it to say. Most people just chose to have it say the first word it spoke during Jobs' presentation: "Hello."

It was fun to have your computer greet you, but there was an important catch: it could not generate an appropriate greeting (or anything else) on its own. It had to be told exactly what to do. If you came home after a great day, your computer would say, "Hello." If you came home after a horrible day, your computer, with the same monotone voice, would say, "Hello." It had no ability to read a situation, answer a question, or figure out the right thing to say at any given time.

A few decades later in 2011, Apple released the iPhone 4S, the first iPhone that came packaged with Siri, Apple's

AI assistant. This, again, was revolutionary. You could talk to your iPhone, and it would respond. You could ask it if you needed a raincoat, and it would tell you that yes, it sure looks like rain today. You could ask it where the nearest pizza place was, and it would give you an address, a phone number, and a link to Yelp reviews. With whatever you said, Siri would attempt to give you an appropriate response.

However, one thing was still missing with Siri (version 1.0): Siri only knew how to respond to you if you told it exactly what you needed. It can't tell how you are feeling on its own. It has no instincts, no ability to read body language, no real clue whether the advice it is giving is actually helpful. Siri's capabilities were impressive. You could argue that this machine, which has no emotions, comes close to achieving some level of emotional intelligence. Nonetheless, there is one thing it lacks, one thing that holds it back from responding to us the way another person could: Awareness.

In 2020, a robotics and AI company called Embodied, Inc. released Moxie, an AI-powered social robot for kids. It is advertised as an emotional companion, and it is programmed to help kids build social skills and self-confidence. Moxie can have full conversations with kids. It picks up on their tone and body language through its microphone and camera, and then it goes into its database and picks the right face to put on, literally. It changes its face, its tone of voice, and the way it engages and interacts with the child based on its perception of how the child is feeling. This, again, represented a big advancement in AI technology. A robot that is not only able to speak and respond to what its user asks it to do but can also use its awareness of the user to figure out the right thing to do on its own. It has incredible processing power, even more than the original Macintosh, and the ability to respond to its user appropriately, similar to Siri. Beyond that, its awareness allows it to know when to use each of those skills. Its awareness allows it to identify and process its own inputs.

The main criticism people have with Moxie and other similar technology is that they have gone too far, that they are *too* human. While many praise the innovation that Moxie represents, some just find it creepy. There have been several movies and episodic shows using AI robots as the antagonists. Movie directors depict the reality of our not-so-distant future as a real-life sci-fi horror. AI-powered devices became a reality when they crossed the chasm of self-learning—this is when the machine selects what inputs it wants, imitating human awareness. Sorry to present AI with a dark context, but the point I really want to make is how important the inputs you look for, gather, and trust are in the process. In other words, how instrumental awareness is.

All of this leads me to the reason I am writing this chapter. It is one of the most important chapters in this book and a big part of the foundation of this sales process. We talk all the time about Intelligence Quotient (IQ), which has been around for a long time. However, we run into a problem when we talk about Emotional Intelligence (typically abbreviated EQ, even though no one calls it "Emotional Quotient"). It has become an all-encompassing term for any and all forms of interpersonal intelligence, so broad that it is often not even helpful. If your boss tells you that they would like you to improve your EQ, are you confident you know exactly what that means, or how you would go about doing it?

I believe we are missing a third key element of human

intelligence. One that is too often lumped in with EQ. It is something we absolutely need if we are truly going to connect with our customers, and it is uniquely *human,* to the point that having a machine attempt to replicate it, is scary. That third element is what I refer to as Awareness Quotient, or AQ. It is a way to quantitatively and even qualitatively measure your awareness, may it be of yourself, your situation, and the person or people you are interacting with. As you will see in the rest of this book, it is absolutely essential to unlocking your full potential as a sales professional.

WHAT IS AWARENESS?

There are two types of awareness: instinctive and cognitive. Instinct is fairly self-explanatory; it is awareness that literally comes without you having to think about it. If someone yells in your face, or if your favorite football team scores a touchdown in the Super Bowl, or if you are on a hike and you see a rattlesnake, you will not have to think about how to respond. Your body is equipped with instinctive awareness for these situations, and these instincts grow over time as you learn and experience more.

Now awareness is not just instinctual; it is also cognitive. You might walk into a conversation without much understanding of how the other person is feeling, but you can pay attention to certain things that will help you figure it out. Using previous experiences and learned knowledge you will be able to identify and key in on certain tell-tells. What is their body language telling you? Are they leaning forward, making eye contact? Are they looking at their watch, shifting their feet to point towards the door? What can you discern from their tone of voice?

When I was selling capital equipment, I spent a lot of time negotiating with key decision-makers. Sitting around a traditional, oversized dark-wood conference room table, the negotiation would officially kick off with someone sliding the first packet of paperwork across the table for all the parties involved to see. Over time, I started to notice every time my negotiations took a turn for the worse, the decision maker who prepared the paperwork would put their hands on the contract and slide it back in front of them as they began to express their dissatisfaction verbally. This was not instinctual to me, it was cognitive. I was making observations and growing my awareness.

See, at a young age, my father taught me in poker, someone who believes they have a strong hand will place their hands on their cards and slightly slide them toward themself, subconsciously protecting them. He was an undercover Special Agent for Customs, and he would also see this behavior from suspects he would encounter who would hold their hand over something of value to them (e.g. a firearm, drugs, etc.).

So how did this help me during negotiations? Well, it let me know that the person who prepared the bid or proposal felt like the other parties at the table were undervaluing something they had prepared. This meant I needed to ask more questions to understand why they were not feeling heard, or why they felt that they needed to protect the paperwork they had prepared. I was able to use it as a trigger to tell myself to ask about it directly. They worked hard preparing it and most of the time did not mind talking about it. I used cognitive awareness to learn more about my customer in these high-stress situations.

Both instinctive and cognitive awareness are important to sales. We work to intentionally learn everything we can from our experiences to grow our instinctual awareness over time. We go into each interaction with a customer with our eyes wide open, knowing what to watch for and pay attention to so that our cognitive awareness is always growing.

When you first meet a customer, you are usually starting from ground zero. You do not know how they will respond to you or your product, what informs their purchasing decisions, or what their feelings are about the product they are currently using. That being said, there are intentional ways you can learn even more about them, ways to be sure you are asking sincere questions, initiating genuine conversations, and actively listening to learn more about them and grow your awareness of their situation. If you sincerely want to understand your customer, you can absolutely grow in this skill set.

While awareness of your customer will always come first, it is also important to grow your awareness of yourself and your process. If you come out of a sales call and the only question you are asking yourself is, "How did it go?", you are not going to end up with any helpful information. You need to dig deeper, be more analytical. You need to intentionally seek awareness of your performance in a sales call based on things that are meaningful to your customer and to your own long-term success. You need to deepen your own understanding of your strengths and weaknesses in relationship to how they can impact a customer. Then assess them in an objective manner.

If you truly want to form connections with your customers and find ways to genuinely help them, you need to prioritize and measure every element of awareness. You need to grow your AQ.

AQ: AWARENESS QUOTIENT

I believe Awareness Quotient, which I will be referring to as "AQ" from here on out, is the third element of human intelligence, along with IQ and EQ.

Most books, workshops, and coaches will just casually lump awareness into EQ. To make it seem like it belongs, they will even attempt to subcategorize it by calling it "Emotional Awareness." Whereas that is just not an accurate representation of what awareness is. Your awareness may prompt you to use your Emotional Intelligence to respond to your customer in a certain way. However, when it comes to awareness itself, there is nothing emotional about it.

Awareness is an input. It is the information you have about the situation you are in. You may have some of that information before entering the situation, and you may gather some in the moment. That is awareness. After you have gathered that information, you use your IQ to process it and determine what to do with it, and your EQ for the best possible response; how to behave in light of what you have learned.

There are lots of people who have the ability to respond to someone in an emotional situation with kindness and empathy, but sometimes those same people have no awareness that the situation calls for empathy in the first place. Everyone has a co-worker who always seems to be unaware of the drama that is unfolding in the office. Or, in a sales atmosphere, you may have a co-worker who misses some pretty obvious buying signals from a potential customer. Nevertheless in both of these situations, when this person is nudged and clued into what is going on, they can adapt fairly quickly and actually help the situation, not only because they care, but because they possess the personal skills we commonly refer to as EQ, even though their awareness (their AQ) is significantly lacking.

IQ is the knowledge you have gained from your past experiences, along with your ability to process new information. AQ is your awareness of your present situation including the people involved (and yourself). EQ is what you are going to do with this information, how you deliver your message in light of your knowledge, experience, and awareness.

In sales, IQ is the "what"—your knowledge, information you recently processed, and the selection of new information you want your customer to know. EQ is the "how"—what delivery style you are going to use to best connect with your customer and help them feel understood. AQ is the input—collection of data coming in from the steady flow of everything you see, hear, feel, and sometimes smell. This data is extremely vital to help you process the "when" and the "who". Understanding *when* to bring up certain points or ask certain questions based on your awareness of how your customer is responding to your message, and knowing *who* they need you to be, which hat you need to put on to best connect with them in this situation.

Because AQ so often gets lumped in with EQ, awareness rarely gets talked about on its own. If you are going to be successful in your career, life, and sales, you will need to be born with a keen sense of awareness or develop your awareness with intentionality and focus. It helps you get to the root of what your customer needs, to be sure you are treating the real cause of their problems instead of just the symptoms. It allows you to see yourself for who you really are and hold yourself accountable for improvement. While it may come more naturally to some people than to others, the good news is that anyone can learn how to develop it and use it to their potential.

Without AQ, we do not have an objective way to measure our observation of a given situation, and we rely too heavily on our own instincts and point of view. I have witnessed several sales calls that have gone poorly, and afterward the sales rep will say, "I think that call went okay. I think the customer is just a late adopter." When I hear a rep say that, I usually find myself waiting for them to laugh or give me a sarcastic smile, because "okay" and "late adopter" do not accurately describe the potential customer or how the sales call went. I also have to remind myself that their "okay" might not be equivalent to my "okay," and their definition of "late adopter" might not match mine, either.

That is why AQ is so important. It gives you a numeric system of Meaningful Measurements (which we will discuss soon) that help you assess your performance and identify areas where you need to grow. It also creates a helpful communication system between sales managers and reps. It is so easy to get lost in semantics, the different definitions we may each have for the terms that we use to evaluate our sales calls. Yet numbers are a universal language, and that is what this system provides. AQ is the number one tool that helped me be successful across all countries and cultures.

If you are using your AQ, you will know…

- **When to offer a suggestion or solution.** If you suggest a solution too soon, and it is a solution your customer does not like, you will lose credibility and remind them that you are a salesperson. You will make them think you only care about making a sale and not about truly understanding their needs.

- **Which direction to steer the conversation.** When the time is right and they know enough about the product along with you knowing enough about them, you want to close the sale by helping them visualize how your product could help them. You do not want to do that too soon. There is truth in the old saying "It's all about the timing." Closing too soon might remove the trust you just gained by understanding them. AQ will help you gauge that timing accurately.
- **When to ask for help or a referral.** If they are not the right customer for you or your product, tell them that. If you have shown yourself to be genuine, you should be able to ask for a referral to a friend or co-worker. Even better, if they are a loyal customer, good awareness will help you to know the right time to ask for their help selling to a colleague or someone else in the same industry.
- **When you need to re-share your message or re-teach your technology.** With good awareness and accurate assessment, you will be able to discern when your customer is misunderstanding a key point about your product, allowing you to tailor your message to focus on what they need from you.
- **How to improve yourself.** Self-awareness is just as important as being aware of your customer. AQ will help you see which of your own behaviors you need to change and even more importantly give you a baseline in which to improve from.

- **When to shut up.** Being aware of when to stop talking and just listen might be the most underrated part of sales, and it is definitely the biggest key to understanding your customer well.

AQ is a practical tool that you can go and use right now. It is not just an abstract idea, you can create and use Meaningful Measurements to equip yourself to get better (more on that in a few pages). Even if you are not looking to revamp your organization's entire sales process, AQ can be added to any existing sales structure to help people in any organization become more aware of the intricate details that made your organization great or will make your organization great!

INWARD AWARENESS

As I have been saying and will continue to say for the rest of this book, sales is all about your customer. It is not about you. Becoming more self-aware is the best way to ignite self-improvement, and the more you improve yourself as a sales professional, the better you will be able to genuinely understand how to best help your customers.

Self-awareness doesn't just apply to sales calls. If you are in a leadership role, it will help you better understand yourself and how you can best lead your employees into a growth mindset by being aware of where you need to grow yourself. It will help you understand your strengths and weaknesses and bring clarity to your backstory, as we discussed in the previous chapter.

Growing in self-awareness takes humility. You have to be willing to look at yourself and acknowledge that, while you have strengths, you also have weaknesses. You have to accept that you are human, that you make mistakes, and that you have blind spots that have kept you from being the best version of yourself. I speak from experience, by the way. I have made lots of mistakes of my own, and I still do. There is no shame in any of this. It just means you are human.

Using AQ and the kind of Meaningful Measurements we are going to talk about later in this chapter will help you grow your self-awareness as a sales professional. There are other resources available to help you with this, too. Personality assessments like the DISC Personality Test, the Myers-Briggs Type Indicator, and the one that I find most practical, the Enneagram. These tools can help you understand yourself in new, meaningful ways that can be helpful in so many areas of your life, including sales.

We all have different ways of processing events, different perspectives on what is most important, and motivations for why we do the things that we do. Personality profiling tools can help you better understand how you see the world. This can be helpful in your everyday life, but it can be particularly helpful in sales. They can teach you to understand the strengths you bring to the table and help you become more aware of your blind spots and how they might impact your interactions with your customers.

I will not go deep into personality profiling in this book, but I'd encourage you to spend time looking into it on your own. I am trained in four different personality profiling systems. I find using something similar to the Enneagram to be the most practical and easiest to remember. There are nine different personality types with the Enneagram, and each one has a different way of processing decisions and different motivations for making those decisions. It can help you get to know yourself and others better by learning their core desires and core fears so you can help them avoid their core fear and accomplish their core desire. The descriptions are short, easy to remember, and most importantly, easy to apply when your awareness picks up that something is not going as planned.

For example, an Enneagram "Three" is driven, highly motivated by goals and success. This can be a very good thing in sales, being strongly motivated can be very helpful. If Three's are not careful, it can also lead to them forgetting about forming a genuine connection with their customer in their pursuit of peak productivity.

On the flipside, an Enneagram "Nine" will likely be very dialed into their customer—what they are thinking, how they are feeling, how much trust is present in their relationship. If Nine's are not careful, this can go to an unhelpful extreme. They can focus so much on their customer that they can lose track of themselves completely and not bring anything of value to the situation, ultimately wasting everyone's time.

Life is a mirror—it doesn't give you what you want, it gives you who you are. Healthy self-questioning will help you see yourself more fully and reduce blind spots, which will help you to keep from getting blindsided. Your goal is not to change who you are. Instead, you have to become more aware of who you are. Find your gifts, embrace your faults, and apply yourself appropriately. Remember, it is vital for you to focus on being *your* best, not being *the* best (please read this sentence one more time).

OUTWARD AWARENESS

Imagine that after your first interaction with a potential customer, they were sent a survey with one single question:

"How well does the sales rep you just visited with truly understand your needs and your overall situation?" Just like on the Newlywed Game from the 70s, I bet your answer would not match their answer.

If you do not understand your customer, you are lost. You will not know how to meet their needs, because you do not have a good reference of where you are or even where you need to go. You will end up making mistakes, making a fool of yourself, and ultimately losing their trust (and their business) as you offer suggestions that do not help them.

Like we have discussed several times, this takes humility. It demands that you practice empathy as you step outside of your own perspective and into your customer's shoes to truly look at the world from their perspective. It means that you have to be humble enough to ask questions, admit to yourself (and even the customer) when you have fallen short in some way, and be willing to work to improve.

Here are a few general rules to keep in mind as you work to build your awareness of your customers:

People think they know more than they actually do.

In human psychology, the Dunning-Kruger effect states that if a person has some surface knowledge about something, they will likely believe that they know more about it than they actually do. For example, if I am trying to sell someone a car that has a safer, more effective anti-lock brake system, I might want to point that out to my customer. Yet if I start the conversation by asking, "This car has a new way of engaging the anti-lock brake system, are you familiar with the new ABS systems?", they might just say yes as a knee-jerk reaction because they know the acronym "ABS" and might have some surface knowledge about what it means, or because they want to seem confident in front of whoever is in the room with them (a co-worker or a spouse, for example). Either way, there is a good chance they have no idea that the ABS system depends on reliable data from speed sensors, which tells a control unit to reduce hydraulic pressure to a single wheel, independently from the other wheels. When they responded "yes" to your question, it took away your opportunity to teach them about a new technology and reinforce how it might benefit them.

You can avoid this by being intentional with the way you bring up the subject in the first place. Rensis Likert is credited not only with coming up with the numeric, satisfied to unsatisfied "Likert Scale", but also the "open-ended" question. Likert used both of these in a clinical setting as a psychologist, but with some tweaks, they both can become very powerful tools to allow you to better understand and help your potential customer.

Mike Fridge at Christian Brothers Automotive uses Likert's numeric satisfaction scale like most companies do to collect important post-sale information. Customer satisfaction surveys are powerful tools to use in your marketing and overall customer experience. The problem with post-sale surveys is that they do not help with the initial sale or the beginning of the sale cycle. What sets Mike's shop apart from other mechanic shops, is that Mike and his team start the sale using Likert's less discussed contribution, the "set up" or the "preface" to the open-ended question. Open-ended questions can be scary to ask sometimes, because the answers often go every direction except the direction you want. Sometimes even worse, if the questions are asked bluntly and the customer gets offended. Hence the reason reps abort asking open-ended questions and replace them with a comment or closed-ended questions. This is also why researchers in the 1800s through 1930s did not use open-ended questions for data collection. Prior to Likert refining the way open-ended questions were structured and applied in clinical settings, the data was unmeasurable and useless.

Good collection of information leads us back to the point I was making with Mike's shop. His sales cycles are relatively short for new customers, and he wants to learn as much about them during their first interaction to ensure they become long-term customers. While the car is in the shop he would also like to repair any other problems or maintenances that are ethically needed. Let's say a customer arrives at his shop knowing at least one thing is broken or needing replacement on their eight-year-old hundred-thousand-mile vehicle. So it's safe to say the initial solution/sale starts off relatively easy. It's the second part where credit is gained or lost. The second part is the mentioning of the other components that are on their last leg and could leave the customer stranded in the near future. A typical close-ended question would sound something like this, "Here is the list of everything we found that is or could become an issue, which ones would you like us to do?"

Now this is how Mike "sets up" or how he "prefaces" his open-ended question. As you read it, please think of how you can apply a similar strategy in your industry. Mike's approach goes something like this…he lets the customer know that they are about to roll their vehicle into the service bay, and then he asks his customers, "As we fix your car, we will most likely notice other components that need attention. I do not want to send the wrong message by mentioning repairs you do not care about. Do you mind telling me a little bit about your car? Do you plan on keeping it forever, or are you thinking of replacing it in a few months?" Prefacing his question like this gives Mike and his team a great understanding of their customers, and it helps them establish a baseline understanding of his customer's awareness and general car knowledge. It provides him with clear indicators of what to share and what kind of education the customer might be open to, which builds credibility with the customer.

So simple to apply, but more importantly, this prefacing prior to the open-ended question builds credibility as much as it removes the risk of offending them. It's pretty common across several different industries for the expert to just point out all the needed repairs and sticker shock the customer with a ridiculous proposal. The expert can be 100% ethical and believe they are just being open and honest with the customer. Meanwhile, the customer feels that the service writer or sales individual absolutely does not understand their needs or situation. This is pure laziness, and it results in the loss of serious credibility.

People need to hear something five times within ninety days to retain most of it.

Hermann Ebbinghaus, a 19th-century German psychologist, developed what we now know as the Ebbinghaus Forgetting Curve, which shows the optimal timeline for sharing information in a way that people will remember. According to this research-backed model, people only remember 50% of what they learn after just one repetition. However, after five repetitions over the course of ninety days, they will remember more than 90%. (Side note: this is just one more example of how important Reasons to Return are; we will be talking more about that soon.)

Every one of us has had to learn something new at some point during our career. It might have been learning the product or service you are selling, the software your company is using, or something else. In any case, you probably didn't learn it with one single demo. Why would we expect anything different with our customers? Think about it this way—you are preventing your customers from learning when you don’t strategize on ways to re-share important information. Help them improve their situation. Find creative ways to repeat and reinforce important industry or product knowledge.

Competition and misinformation.

Ebbinghaus’s model was not developed specifically for sales professionals, so it makes sense that he didn’t take into account the impact of competition or distractions when he developed it. In most cases, dealing with competition will make retention rates even lower. You might have your timeline laid out, your messaging clear, your plan in place, and then come in one day to find that your customer now believes something about your product that just is not true, something your competition told them. Your competition can muddy the waters and confuse your messaging with theirs. Sometimes this can even happen as the result of an uninformed co-worker or friend giving them inaccurate information unintentionally. Being aware of this ahead of time will help you strategize against it and be ready to adapt when it happens.

The more consistent you are, the more trust you build.

When customers know what to expect from you, it helps them build trust in you. If you bring a consistent customer-focused approach each time you visit, they will start to feel more confident that they know what to expect from you. Yet if you are erratic in your communication, not following through with little promises, showing up with different random ideas that do not fit their needs, they will feel off-balance and unsure of what to expect from you. They will keep their guard up, and it will be almost impossible to form a meaningful connection with them.

Not every product is right for every person.

Part of your responsibility as a sales professional is to make sure that any product you are selling to a customer is the *right* product for them. If you truly want what's best for them, then you need to have their back. A big part of building your awareness of them is understanding their situation well enough to know whether your product will be the right fit. When I worked for Rent-a-Center, I didn't want my customers to choose a piece of furniture that was too expensive for their budget. I didn't want them to find themselves in a position where they wouldn't be able to pay for the piece they had chosen and end up having it repossessed by me. I had witnessed this happening several times, once even in front of a customer's kids, and it broke my heart. I never wanted anyone else to have to go through that. I was going to protect them from overspending. After that, there were many times when a customer would be looking at a certain piece of furniture, and I would literally tell them, "Let me show you a better deal. I don't think you will be happy with that one. Let me show you the piece I would buy if I were you." It built trust, and because my job was to verify their employment and income, I know I saved several people from embarrassment in front of their family.

Being aware of your customer, going into every interaction with eyes wide open, is critical. Building that awareness in a meaningful way takes intentionality and work. It takes a system that equips you to keep track of the things that are most meaningful to you and (especially) your customer in this process.

It takes one of the most important pieces of the process of growing your AQ: Meaningful Measurements.

MEANINGFUL MEASUREMENTS

What gets measured gets improved. It is something I learned at a young age, and it is something I have seen to be true in many ways over the years, both in sales and in life.

My son was a competitive swimmer in high school, ranked highly in the state. His coach preached repetition. Building muscle memory by practicing the same mechanics over and over, so many times that his swimmers looked the same during practice as they did during a swim meet. He was a good coach, and his approach was smart. Except, only if his swimmers were practicing the correct technique.

This became an issue for my son. He was winning, so he kept practicing the same way, over and over again. However, he had one bad habit: he was not fully rotating his palm, when it was out of the water, during his backstroke. So with every practice rep, he solidified a bad habit further into place. At first, this was no big deal, but after thousands of reps over years of swimming, his relentless practice of a poor technique served to reinforce his poor form and, more importantly, eat away at his shoulder joint. Once the pain started and we realized the issue, he had already built up scar tissue in his shoulder, along with a serious bad habit.

Looking back, I wish I had been more concerned with measurements of quality and technique than I was with the results of his races and his many laps in the fast lane at practice. My son was everything you want in an athlete. He worked hard, had a great attitude, was extremely coachable, wanting to improve, and willing to push through the pain. Which he did, pain that was not needed for his success. If we had measured what really mattered, not the results, but the technique that led to them, we could have helped him improve in a way that would have benefitted him long-term.

I have had several conversations with sales managers over the years about how to measure the "it factor," what skills make a particular sales rep good. What is the equivalent of a properly executed backstroke for a sales professional? How do we track, not the results, but the technique and approach that leads to consistent, sustainable success and helps grow awareness of areas that need improvement?

Ultimately, the answers I have received have been unsatisfying. Some might talk about drive, how important it is for a sales rep to be strongly motivated to do well. Though that is true, of course, it feels incomplete. Lots of people have the drive to succeed, but crash and burn anyway. Alternately, people would usually just say the skills that make a successful sales rep are subjective, impossible to quantify or measure in a consistent way.

Those answers just were not satisfactory to me. Why do we not have a system to measure these skills (even if they are subjective) a system that can be tailored to different sales professionals to measure the strengths that give them the potential to be great? Why is there not a way to help sales professionals become more aware of their own behaviors that are producing results, good or bad?

That is why I created the concept of Meaningful Measurements and AQ. Like the information a doctor gets by monitoring a patient's vital signs in a hospital, Meaningful Measurements will help you keep track of how you are doing in the places that matter most to your success: your ability to ask questions that get you as much information as possible, your ability to offer a solution as close to the customers' exact needs as possible, to show initiative, gain trust, and more. They allow you to measure your performance and technique, and they help you establish a numeric baseline to improve from. Being able to describe your skill set out loud means nothing if you do not have a way to measure your progress. That is exactly what this system is for.

Using this system is simple: you just identify a specific area of AQ that you want to track, measure, and improve, and then you rate yourself on a scale from 0-10 after each sales call. You can start small—the first time you use this system, just pick one thing to measure. Then, as you grow more comfortable, add more. Make them unique to your industry based on the needs most important to you or your customer. Track them over time to see your own growth and better understand what areas you need to improve.

These Meaningful Measurements come in the form of questions. Honesty is required here. If you are not willing to judge yourself honestly, this system is not going to help you. Now if you are willing to be real with yourself and you have a growth mindset, Meaningful Measurements will help take you to the next level.

Here are some of the most common Meaningful Measurements to get you started. You can certainly come up with your own or use variations of these, but this will help you track the elements of AQ that I have generally found to be most important.

Self Awareness

On a scale of 0—10 . . .

- How well did you teach the differences in your technology / process?
- How important or valuable is what you learned about your customer today?
- How well do you understand your customer's concerns or largest pain point?
- How memorable were you?
- How much influence do you hold over their decisions now?
- How much value did you bring today?

Customer Awareness

On a scale of 0—10 . . .

- How interested was your customer in meeting with you?
- How interested were they in the idea of you returning?
- How attentive were they to the information you shared?
- How much information did they retain from your last meeting?

- How much do they trust your messaging?
- How much do they trust you?

Situational Awareness
On a scale of 0—10…

- How impactful will your product be to your customer's situation?
- How well does the customer recognize the severity of their current situation?
- How much benefit do they envision your solution delivering?
- How much value did you bring, or do you bring to this account overall?

Fair warning: this process may be humbling at first, but stick with it. Start small, and set your sights on growth. Once you have set some AQ values as a baseline to grow from, seeing yourself grow and improve over time will build your confidence as a sales professional. Measurable growth is more than just important for improved performance, it is a great self-esteem builder, too.

I want to give you an example, to show you how this could play out in practice by telling you how it played out for me in a series of sales calls I had with a doctor I sold to. I focused on four Meaningful Measurements to evaluate my interactions with this doctor:

- How much did he trust me?
- How well did I understand him?
- How much of his attention had I captured?
- How much of my messaging did he retain?

I tracked these questions on a scale from 0-10 across each interaction, and it helped me understand what I needed to do to best meet his needs. Here is what that looked like in practice:

FIRST VISIT:

- Trust: 0. He didn't know me, so I had not gained any of his trust.
- Understanding: 1. I had not met him, but I understood a bit about him from asking others who knew him.
- Attention: 8. He was not comfortable around me or with my product, so I had a lot of his attention.
- Retention: 0. He didn't have any understanding of our company's messaging or technology yet at this point.

SECOND VISIT:

- Trust: 2. He began to trust me a bit more—determined by his body language and his acceptance of the product claims I made.
- Understanding: 2. I was understanding him a bit better through the questions he was asking and the side conversations he'd have with his staff that I'd observe during our meeting.
- Attention: 7. He was getting more familiar with me, and I noticed that he was giving me less of his attention. There were small indications of this, like his eye contact decreasing.

- Retention: 1. His retention still was not high, but it was starting to increase a little bit.

THIRD VISIT:

- Trust: 3. I could see that his trust was truly starting to increase at this point. At times, he would ask a question on behalf of one of his nurses and let me give them the answer, not interrupting or correcting me at all.
- Understanding: 4. I was understanding him better as we spent more time together.
- Attention: 4. I noticed a significant drop in the doctor's attention on this visit. He was filling out patients' charts, talking to patients and staff, and even eating while we met. His attention really dropped off because he was more familiar with me.
- Retention: 2. He was gradually beginning to retain more of our messaging.

FOURTH VISIT:

- Trust: 4. On this visit, the doctor began letting me talk to patients about their procedure before he even did. I could tell that his trust in me was continuing to increase. However, that was not the case for any of my other Meaningful Measurements . . .
- Understanding: 4. My understanding of the doctor remained flat this meeting, because rather than continuing forward in the process we had

already started, we had to back up a bit. A competitor had come in and made some false claims about how their product compared to ours, so I had to focus this meeting on circling back and reestablishing the foundation we had built in our previous interactions.
- Attention: 3. Unfortunately, even as I dealt with the curveball my competition had thrown me, the doctor's attention in what I was saying continued to fade.
- Retention: 1. His retention of our messaging had dropped due to the murky waters the competition had led him into.

FIFTH VISIT

- Trust: 6. This was a turning point. He had scheduled a few trial cases over the period of time we had been meeting together, and the good results of those cases combined with the reeducation we had worked on during my fourth visit resulted in a big jump in trust and complete loyalty. He never let the competition schedule another lunch-and-learn for his office. Not only did my trust go up, but their trust dropped when the physician researched the rep's false claims.
- Understanding: 6. After all we had been through and all the time we'd spent together, my understanding of him was at its peak.
- Attention: 2. His attention on me continued to drop. On this visit he barely made eye contact with me. (This would turn out to be a normal

trait, but I was totally fine with it because for the next eleven years, he was 100% loyal and a great doctor to work with.)

- Retention: 3. His retention of our messaging had begun to rebound.

Your sales process will look different with each customer you engage with. Nonetheless, the ups and downs in the process I went through with this doctor are normal, and they are a great example of why AQ is so important. Because I started applying AQ relatively early in this situation, I was able to start applying corrections fairly early in the process, capturing more of his attention with interesting and meaningful information and increasing his retention by revisiting the same product features and benefits but just delivering it in different ways. Not only did he end up being loyal for eleven years, but he also tripled his volume with me.

AQ can be a game-changer, but to build your awareness, you have to measure it. You have to become aware of your awareness itself, to understand where you are and where you need to grow.

So, put AQ into practice. Create some of your own measurements or steal the measurements I just listed and use them for yourself or your sales team. The best way to start applying AQ is to keep it simple and pick two Meaningful Measurements that you feel will be most beneficial to your understanding of your customer. Then come up with something that will continuously remind you to assess the sales call. (I call these cognitive triggers, and we will dive deeper into how to use them with customers later in the book.) I personally used my car as a cognitive trigger—the second I walked out of someone's office, house, or restaurant, sat in my car, and felt the air conditioner kick on, I would immediately assess the sales call and score my Meaningful Measurements. Commit to making it part of the way you end every sales call, and eventually, it will become a habit.

WHO TO BE

One last benefit of growing your awareness is that it will give you a clearer picture of who your customer needs you to be. You will be able to better discern what they need from you in order to be ready to join you on the journey.

Do not hear this as me saying you should be inauthentic. As I have said many times in this book, my goal is to help you become the best version of *yourself* as a sales rep. The core answer of "who to be" is always the same: be you.

Remember this, it is okay to step into different roles in a given sales call, depending on the customer you are working with, much like the way we take on different patterns of behaviors in different areas and relationships within our own lives. The way I talk to my spouse is different from how I talk to my dad, or my boss, or another co-worker. This is situational, and having the emotional depth to be present, empathetic, and impactful is demonstrating strong EQ. You'd certainly behave differently around a friend during a casual lunch verses helping that same friend going through a divorce.

That is why I find the phrase "who to be" so useful. It gives you clarity on what role you are adopting in each situation that you find yourself in, and that will make it much easier for you to determine what to do. You may become aware that your customer needs you to be…

- **The Consultant.** If you are working with someone who's not very experienced in the area you are selling (e.g. virus protection software or retirement planning), they may look to you as a source of industry knowledge and expertise.
- **The Humble Student.** On the flip side, if someone is extremely experienced in the product or service field, possibly even enough of an expert to speak at a national convention for the industry you sell in (e.g. a highly experienced and well-published neurosurgeon), they will value your humility and willingness to learn. It wouldn't make sense for you to pretend you know more than they do because you do not. You will learn more from them than anyone else, and it will deepen your relationship with them. Plus, in the role of a student, you can ask any question you want, and those questions can often prompt new ideas and good discussion with your customer.
- **The Teacher.** With new technology, you will have times when you will need to train your customer on what you are selling. Even if they know more about their area of expertise than you do, you will need to be ready to teach them how to use the product in a way that helps them eventually feel like an expert.
- **The Valued Friend.** As we have discussed, most customers are not actively looking for a new friend. So being "too friendly" can put a lot of people off. However, other times, you will encounter people with whom you genuinely connect and who enjoy hanging out with you

socially. These relationships start with trust; they feel you have their back and best interest at heart. Do not get lazy. Continue to bring them industry information to help them be their best. Be a good friend, not just a fun one.

- **The Loyal Soldier.** As you meet different customers, you will encounter some who are highly driven, running large organizations, moving fast, making quick requests of vendors that they believe are competent. They operate like a general on a battlefield, and the best way to relate with them is to be their loyal soldier. These personalities types (D in DISC personality profile and #8 in the Enneagram) usually have a small circle of trust, and if you are inside it, they'll be loyal to you as long as you can keep up and are loyal to them. They're also very protective of the individuals in their circle of trust and will help you grow your business by heavily encouraging others to buy from you.
- **The Sales Rep.** There is a time and place to act like a "typical" sales rep, asking closing questions, working out the specifics of a sale, etc. Be cautious. Only shift into this role when the time is right. The more time you can spend focused on your customer's needs rather than the sale itself, the more powerful your interaction will be.

Every single interaction you have with your customer should be all about them. How are they feeling about you and your product? What do they need from you? Who do they need you to be? If you intentionally use AQ quantified by Meaningful Measurements, you will be able to figure out the answers to these questions and more. You will understand what you need to do to help them be successful. You will put yourself in a position to make them the hero, which will in turn put you on the leaderboard.

CHAPTER 6
THE S.A.L.E.S PROCESS

DURING THE TRANSITION TO MY INTERNATIONAL SALES execution role, I received some great advice from two different individuals around the same time, which made me really take notice.

First, my president at the time, Maulik, said, "As you work with individuals in these countries, do not just tell them your solution, help them find their solution." I love this quote; it is so powerful! Not only do I apply this in coaching, but I try to apply it with all my relationships.

Second, I received confirmation of that message as Tom Collard, my long-time trusted colleague and company's VP of International Business Development, reinforced the same message (with a little personal touch added). He said, "Be careful; do not go around telling all the international reps how the American guy would do it, especially some guy from the bayous of Louisiana. They don't have your skillset. Find the best way for them to do it." At first, I was confused with this advice because I thought they wanted me to share my style and my experiences. Was this not the reason why they selected me for this position?

After a few weeks abroad in Australia and then Germany, I quickly realized how spot-on they both were. Their words of wisdom immediately put me in a humble, observational mindset. I started putting into practice that old saying, "You have two ears and one mouth for a reason," and I saw for myself just how much value there was in what they shared.

Think about it. Imagine this advice applied in your own territory and industry. It applies everywhere. The exact way you sell will not work for someone else who has a completely different personality. You can't tell someone to just be funny if you are gifted with humor and they are not. You can't tell a naturally soft-spoken person to be more aggressive just because that style works for you. I can't believe this advice is not shared more often amongst peers on the same team.

Sales advice or a sales process that forces someone to do things that are not natural for them will not work. It will not empower them to lean into their strengths, and it will not be sustainable long term. Every sales professional needs a system that focuses on the most important core traits while allowing them to stay true to themselves.

With my heightened sense of awareness in play, it was not long before I started identifying cross-cultural sales traits and skill sets that all the top reps around the world possessed, things that successful sales professionals have in common, no matter where in the world they are selling or who they are selling to. Yes, there are some large cultural differences, but after the initial unique cultural greetings, you quickly realize we have a lot more in common than we do in difference. One being that a connection is a connection and genuine connections drive genuine results.

Focusing on everything we have in common to make a

meaningful connection. That is what my sales process does. It is the reason I wrote this book, and it is what we will be focusing on from here on out. This process will lead you through steps I have seen work with customers time and time again, but it will also leave you room to lean into your own strengths and focus on the value you uniquely bring to the sales process. It will help you become the best version of yourself as a sales professional.

ONE-SIZE-FITS-ONE

One big difference between my sales approach and others you may have encountered is that I am going to advise you to wait as long as possible before offering your customer a solution. Many books will tell you to offer solutions early and often, have rehearsed bullet points ready to go, and work to overcome your customer's objections as quickly as possible. Even if you read a book that doesn't want you to offer solutions immediately, they will most likely want you to ask questions that sound open-ended but are not, because the questions are directed toward the specific solution you want to offer, a predetermined solution.

You are not going to find any of that here. It is more important to understand your customer's objections than to quickly overcome them. We are not about treating symptoms. We are about uncovering the root cause, listening to understand your customer, and guiding them to a vision of how *they* can be the hero in their own story, the one who chooses the solution and makes things better for themselves and their entire team.

Sales is not one-size-fits-all. It is *one-size-fits-one*. The way you sell needs to be unique to you, and the way you approach each customer needs to be unique to them. It takes practice and thoughtfulness to use this approach well, but if you commit to it, you will build the kind of meaningful, lasting connections you need with your customers. They will understand that you care about them, and you will be able to help them solve their problems because you will have the ability to uncover and genuinely understand what their problems are.

Before we dive into the steps of the SALES process itself, I want to share a story about one of the most knowledgeable doctors I have ever worked with, Dr. Yearwood. He would probably cringe knowing that I am mentioning sales in the same sentence as healthcare. Yet in my opinion, good doctors practice the most pure form of sales: understanding their patients, unearthing the root of their problems, and helping them understand how the treatment plan they recommend will help lead them to a better place. In a lot of ways, we could think about modeling our sales approach after good doctors, and Dr. Yearwood is an excellent example.

Almost all industries have customers that shop around. Medicine is no different. The doctors I worked with would often have patients who would doctor-shop. If a doctor was not meeting the patient's expectations after two or three minor procedures, they would look elsewhere, even if the doctor was good and technically doing everything correctly. It was very common for patients to question their doctor and hesitate to agree to another procedure if their last procedure had not met the patient's expectations. It might take something significant like a bad pain flare-up before they would agree to schedule another procedure, even if the procedure was fairly minor.

However, when I started working with Dr. Yearwood, I noticed right away that this didn't happen to him. His patients stayed with him, not only past the first couple of appointments, but for years and years after. When Dr. Yearwood suggested to them a procedure, even a larger one, they agreed to it without hesitation. He seemed to have a way of earning the complete trust and loyalty of his patients.

What made Dr. Yearwood so different? He put the patient first, one hundred percent of the time. He took the time to re-examine their pain, get hands-on with them, and reconfirm that his original assessment, months earlier, was correct, which made his patients feel like he really knew what was going on. When there was a problem, he educated them to make sure they understood it. When they shared personal goals and expectations, he took them seriously. He always had a plan, and he always communicated his plan with his patients. This plan was not only for their next procedure, but also for what he planned to do if there was still lingering pain after this procedure. His patients felt understood, and they felt like there was someone in their corner who was competent and truly cared about them.

Each step of the process mattered to Dr. Yearwood. He was never in a rush to get to the end. What mattered to him was not just finding a solution, but finding the *right* solution. A solution that addressed his patient's core issue. His priority was always his patient.

If you are going to successfully put this sales approach into practice, that needs to be your mindset, too. You have to stay committed to each part of the process, prioritizing the customer every step of the way, not looking for shortcuts or easy workarounds to make a quick sale at the expense of your consumer's real need. You have to shift your focus from macro ("I am going to get this sale!") to micro ("I am going to focus on the task at hand").

If you want to sell more and do it with less stress while building a fan base of customers to help you explode with referrals, then I recommend taking in and committing to the process below. The return on investment is well worth your effort.

THE S.A.L.E.S PROCESS

Over the next five chapters, I am going to give you an overview of each of the five steps of the sales process. I will summarize them briefly here:

- **Strategize** - Before every interaction with your customer, make a plan. Be aware of your goals. Understand big-picture goals and the need for continuous interactions. Prepare multiple ideas for the next Reason to Return (future follow-up).
- **Articulate your message** - Share information that is both meaningful and interesting to your customer to gain their attention and maximize their retention. Share content that promotes honest dialog. Understand them; don't interrupt them.
- **Listen and learn** - After you have shared your message, shut up and listen. Take the opportunity to learn from them.
- **Explore emotions** - When the time is right, dive deeper into the issues your customer is facing, and help them envision a situation where they see themselves as the hero because they chose your product.

- **Solidify** - Secure a commitment from your customer, identify next steps, and place cognitive triggers.

If you commit to this process, even your "bad" sales calls will have something good come out of them. It can be a real game-changer for you, especially when it comes to finding out the real reasons why potential customers are reluctant to sign on the dotted line.

CHAPTER 7
STRATEGIZE

I AM NOT A GREAT CHESS PLAYER. I ENJOY IT, AND I understand the strategy of the game. When I play chess, I play maybe two moves ahead at a time. I make my move, I wait for my opponent to make their move, and then I re-evaluate my next two moves.

However, for the best chess players in the world, the game looks totally different. They are not strategizing move-by-move. When they look at a chess board, they are seeing four or even five moves ahead. They take into account their opponent's most likely decisions so they will know how to respond and put themselves in a position to win. It is what separates elite chess players from those of us who just play for fun.

In your sales calls, how many moves ahead are you? Are you making your decisions reactively, just going with the flow? Are you making all of your decisions on the fly, making it up as you go along, trusting your instincts and your ability to "wing it"? Or are you going in with a solid Plan A and Plan B, strategizing intentionally so that you are putting yourself in the best position and fully leveraging your strengths?

I have seen the whole spectrum of different preparation styles among the sales reps I've worked with. Some prepare in excruciating detail for many days leading up to a sales call. Some save their prep for the parking lot minutes before the call itself. Different levels of preparation are okay, and the level of preparation needed can vary across different industries. Nonetheless, if you are going to succeed, you have to strategize. I have encountered reps who do not prepare at all. These reps usually tell me "we are going to stop in and see how they are doing." Not a good strategy, horrible for sustained success or growth.

The amount of thought and strategy you devote to your sales calls beforehand is directly related to your industry and your personality. If you spend too much time preparing you might suffer from paralysis by analysis. If you don't strategize, then learn to. There needs to be a happy medium, an amount of prep that you are comfortable with and yields results. This applies differently across different industries, but it always matters. Get your thoughts and material together, know your micro moves that will get you to your macro goal. That's what I mean when I talk about being prepared. If you are in retail sales, your strategy will be applied on your first follow-up call, after you have engaged with your customer for the first time. Regardless of your situation, if you care about meeting your customer's needs, you need to strategize. You need to be planning for what meaningful information you can share with them, what specific goals you have for the interaction itself, and how you are going to create a compelling reason that will allow a follow-up interaction. It's how you position yourself for success, and bring your customer as much value as possible.

WHY STRATEGY MATTERS

One thing I have observed among the best sales reps: they do little things in a sales call that far exceed what was expected of them. Potential customers will notice, and even if they don't buy from you, they will have no problem giving you a strong referral.

Many of these successful reps have profound awareness and can respond well to their customers during a sales call. Yet that is not the main reason they're able to consistently raise the bar for what success looks like. The key is the way they set themselves up for success beforehand. Before the sales call starts, when they are under no time constraints, no pressure or expectations from the customer or their manager or anyone else, they take the time to think through multiple potential scenarios so they will be ready for anything. This allows them to envision their potential next moves and establish their goals. They win because they take a few minutes to strategize various possibilities and scenarios. Before every Olympic race, swimmer Michael Phelps doesn't just envision himself winning. He also visualizes any and everything that could go wrong. By anticipating unexpected setbacks, he ensures he is never caught off guard. He even knows what to do because he has already given it thought.

An important point to remember is that in sales, it is never just you and your customer. There will always be other factors stealing their attention, impacting their thought process, creating biases, and influencing their motivations and decisions. On top of that, there will be other sales reps pushing other products and services, other people who will be impacted by their decision, and other external factors on their mind that you might not be aware of. The marketplace is full of misinformation and noise that will make it more difficult for you to connect with your customer and share your message effectively. You have to go into each sales call with eyes wide open to all of this, ready with goals to help you measure success, intentional messaging tailored for your situation, and a plan for how to respond if things do not go the way you think they will.

If you put in the effort and go through all these scenarios in your head as you prepare before the sales call, your potential goes through the roof. You will reduce the pressure of hoping everything goes perfect, allowing yourself to truly focus on your customer and their needs. Also, you will keep yourself from being thrown off balance by anything in the sales call, allowing you to share your message effectively and secure a meaningful Reason to Return.

INTENTIONAL MESSAGING

When forming your strategy, the first questions you are going to ask yourself are obvious: What are you going to talk about? What are you going to open with? How are you going to start the conversation?

Remember that your goal is not to get your customer to the finish line as fast as humanly possible. It's to be proactive and thorough as you work to find the best solution for your customer. If you are preparing for your first meeting with your customer, you should also be thinking about your second and third meeting with them. Remember they are not going to retain everything in a single meeting.

Strategize for today thinking about future meetings. You want the material and information you share to build off of each other. You also want to make sure what you share is interesting and meaningful. Educate and share in moderation. Sharing too much information at once reduces retention of your message. Sorry to sound like a broken record, but being intentional with the amount you share will leave you with meaningful information to share on future visits. Help them focus on retaining what you really want them to remember. You really want to help them create a solid foundation of knowledge, giving you a place to build from with repetition in your future meetings. Also, the less you share gives them an opportunity to speak and for you to learn.

If this is your first sales call, it is a good idea to start with a quick version of your story (backstory + new story, like we discussed in chapter four), some background on your company, or something new in the industry. Going in with a plan like this will give you a solid and meaningful way to break the ice and help them understand who you are.

The messaging you select should fit into a very small window of time (two minutes or less is ideal) and then set yourself up to listen and learn. This makes intentionality even more important. You need to make the most of this small window of time, those precious moments when you actually have their full attention. Your message needs to be meaningful, relevant, and interesting to them, and it needs to be in line with your goals for this specific sales call and for your journey with this customer overall.

Here are a few things to keep in mind as you select your messaging for your next sales call:

- **Expect curve balls.** Sales calls are full of surprises, so flexibility is important. Go in with the understanding that your customer may not respond to your message in the way you had expected. Maybe you will share an interesting case study written by an author they do not like or a piece of data that they seem thoroughly unimpressed by. Fortune favors the prepared, and with intentional time spent preparing your message beforehand, you can equip yourself to make quick adjustments on the fly when you need to.
- **Remember the forgetting curve.** Ebbinghaus's Forgetting Curve is a huge factor you need to keep in mind when selecting your messaging. If you want your customer to retain your message long-term, you are going to need to share it with them across multiple visits. Remember that if today is their first time hearing your message, they will most likely forget half of it by tomorrow. You need to structure your message over multiple visits in a way that will build a foundation of learning for your customer and help them retain the most important information over time.
- **Everyone makes mistakes.** Do everything you can to set yourself up for success. Do not expect yourself to be perfect. As you are planning, take time to think about what might happen if you make a mistake. How are you going to respond if your customer calls you out on a detail you get wrong? What are you going to do if your words come out the wrong way? Mistakes are never the

goal, but if you prepare well, they do not have to be fatal, either. And they can be great opportunities to display true humility to your customer.

- **Bring value every single time.** Never forget that whenever you meet with a customer, they are giving you something valuable, their time. So, it is absolutely essential that you attempt to give them something of value in return. This can look a lot of different ways. It could be a case study that is relevant to them, information from a conference or seminar in their industry, a partial product demo to help them understand how your product could impact them in a positive way, or something else that you believe is right for your customer. No matter the specifics, for them to want you to come back, you have to show them you value their time by sharing something meaningful and interesting.
- **Be predictable.** Predictability is a way to build trust with your customer, as long as it is the right kind of predictability. So, make it your goal to display positive, predictable behavior that the customer recognizes. When the customer sees you, you want them to know immediately that they are about to hear some new info or learn something new today. Either way, you want them to know you are bringing it, and "it" is value.

REASONS TO RETURN

As we discussed near the beginning of this book, creating compelling Reasons to Return is the secret sauce to my entire sales method. It is the one constant I have observed in every single good sales rep I have worked with across the globe. You can only win the game if you are in the game, and creating interesting and meaningful Reasons to Return will keep you in the game.

Imagine you are on a first date with someone you're really interested in having a long-term relationship with. It wouldn't be very smart to get to the end of a magical first date and just say, "Okay, see you later!", hoping for the best. If you really feel like they're the one, you need to have a plan to secure a second date before saying goodbye. The best way to do this is by showing up to the first date with at least three ideas for a second date.

During your first date, you might learn from your date that they hate sand, so you don't suggest your idea of a romantic walk on the beach. Then, you might learn that their dog doesn't play well with other dogs, so you scratch your dog park date idea. Thank goodness you had a third idea: a hiking trail that would be appropriate for their dog. You put yourself in a much better position to keep things going with them because you came prepared with multiple ideas and focused on what mattered to them the most. Not only did you give them something to look forward to, but you also gave them something to talk to their friends about.

It's the same with sales. Imagine you go into an initial sales call with a potential customer assuming the second sales call will be an exciting demo of your newest product, only to have your potential customer say "no thank you, just leave a brochure." You are totally caught off guard, as they answer a call and wave goodbye. It was going so well; they seemed so interested. Hopefully, I have made it obvious how important securing a second sales interaction is. Well, not to complicate things, but I need to reinforce how this second sales interaction needs to be interesting and meaningful, too. Otherwise, there is a high probability that you will receive a text or email canceling your follow-up appointment a day before the appointment.

On my first sales call with Dr. Yearwood, he flat-out told me that he was not going to use my product because of his specialized technique that he could only perform with the system he used. His outright and confident rejection of my product caught my attention and sparked my curiosity. So, I asked him to elaborate, which he did in great detail. It became obvious quickly that Dr. Yearwood was a teacher at heart. I really wanted to secure a Reason to Return, but his hard "no" toward using my product burned through the first two ideas I had come prepared with. Keep in mind this hard "no" came after seven hours in his patient lobby waiting to see him and being told three times by his gatekeeper that he would not be able to see me that day or any other day (a story for another time).

So, I had to resort to number three, which was requesting that he allow me to observe him doing other procedures that had nothing to do with my product but would help me learn about the industry. Dr. Yearwood loved to teach, so it was easy and natural for me to take on the role of a humble student. I was new to the industry, so I knew without a doubt I could benefit from his teaching. I had nothing to lose by asking him to let me shadow him, and it was a very low-stress request to make, because he had already made it clear that I would not be "selling" him. Wow, this last-ditch effort ended up being a Masterclass of Pain Medicine, I felt like I was enrolled in an accelerated Medical Degree. My sincere desire to learn from him allowed him to know the real me, which helped form trust both ways, and ultimately formed a great friendship.

I did ultimately earn his business. It took me nine months, but from that point forward, we worked together exclusively for the next eleven years. The real victory came from the knowledge he passed on to me. I am still his student to this day, twenty years later, and I refer to him as my "work Dad." Vocationally, I have never learned so much from one person in my life as I did from him. Dr. Yearwood has since moved to London, and even though it has been close to decade since I was his sales rep, we still talk frequently and meet in person at least twice a year. I'm still learning from him, and in return, this loyal student asks a lot of challenging questions that have sparked a lot of creative ideas in his head.

I could have easily and justifiably given up in my first meeting with Dr. Yearwood when my first few ideas for a Reason to Return completely missed the mark. It makes me smile thinking about how meaningful and impactful it was for me to find a way to stay in the game. That is the power of Reasons to Return. As long as you give yourself a strong Reason to Return, re-engaging with meaning, you are still in the game. If you can continuously find ways to do this, you are going to win. It is like being given the power to put time back on the clock at the end of a basketball game, or move the chains on every fourth down of a football game. Reasons to Return keep you moving forward. Believe that when it comes to sales, if you stay in the game, you are eventually going to win.

For anyone thinking this is not true, maybe you are even calling me out right now, "Travis, this is so wrong, I have lost several deals where the bid is closed or the customer inked the deal with my competition. The deal is absolutely lost." I would tell you, in the short run maybe so. I would quickly follow up with, "How much value did you bring?" Enough to earn three or four strong referrals? Enough to be promised the next deal? Enough to put serious pressure on the rep that won the deal? When you realized that you might not get the deal, did you start strategizing for referrals, their next bid, or to be a contingency plan if the other product/rep didn't deliver on their promises? However, in the future, they may come back to you and become a customer testimony for you, vocalizing why they should have gone with you in the first place.

European hospitals tend to use tenders (bids) way more often than hospitals in the US, Latin America, the Middle East, or Asia Pacific. In a situation where a tender has been awarded, the physician does not have the freedom to select the product they feel will best treat a particular patient. These tenders lock the losing vendors out for two years. I have been coaching the same reps in Europe and Nordics long enough to observe them lose the initial battle, but come back and win the war. They were all playing the long game. Every one of them will attest to the importance of strategizing interesting and meaningful Reasons to Return. I could fill an entire book with inspiring stories from the reps I coach, detailing their significant victories achieved by strategically playing the long game.

Now, the magic behind Reasons to Return is not just about repetition. Your customer is not going to automatically decide to buy from you just because they see you on a regular basis. The reason this works is because of what is happening behind the scenes. When you find interesting and meaningful Reasons to Return, you are intentionally increasing positive exposure to your customer, which gives you a chance to **earn their trust, understand their needs,** and **get the solution right**. You are not just showing up again and again to show them more stuff. You are building trust, deepening your connection across multiple visits, and working to learn how you can be most helpful to them.

This is a great place to bring AQ into your strategy as well. If Reasons to Return are something you want to work on, then ask yourself at the end of each sales call: on a scale of 0—10…

- How interested was the customer in the return visit I suggested?
- How well did I set up a meaningful Reason to Return today?
- How prepared was I with multiple possibilities to respond to their needs or interests?
- It's a skill that you can grow over time with intentional focus.

Finding the right balance is the biggest thing to watch out for when setting up a Reason to Return: you want your customer to view you as persistent, but never as aggravating. Your goal is to keep it interesting for them, to return for reasons that they will find appealing and meaningful. You are trying to eventually wear down their resistance, but you do not want to wear *them* down and bring them to a place where they are tired of seeing you.

So how do we do this? The same way we do everything in sales: by putting the customer first. Use what you know about them (and what you are always continuing to learn about them) to figure out what Reasons to Return would be most meaningful to them. Hunt for anything they are interested in or any common ground you might share. The very best thing you can do is to go into your meeting with at least three potential Reasons to Return in mind. Use whatever you may know about your customer to come up with potential reasons, so you do not have to come up with them on the fly.

This is important for a couple of key reasons, the more obvious being that having these ideas in advance will safeguard you from getting into a situation where the one idea you share doesn't appeal to your customer. Yet there is another less obvious reason, and it is even more important: if you go into your meeting prepared with multiple potential Reasons to Return, you are actually forcing yourself into a position where you have no choice but to listen. If your ultimate goal is to set up a return visit, you will be listening to everything your customer says to evaluate which of your potential Reasons to Return will be most meaningful and interesting to them. You will be a better listener, truly taking in everything they say rather than just waiting for your turn to talk. You will be dialed in, and you will leave the meeting with more than just a Reason to Return that is meaningful to them. You will also have a much deeper understanding of who they are and what they value.

As I have already said a few times in this chapter, Reasons to Return need to be two things: interesting and meaningful. Your customer needs to view your Reason to Return as a good use of their time, and it needs to be meaningful to them and (ideally) the sale you are hoping to eventually make. This can take many different forms, and like everything, it needs to be based around your knowledge of your customer. So feel free to get creative! To get you started, here are a few examples of what compelling Reasons to Return might look like:

- **Product demonstrations** - If they are interested in your product, offer to come back and do a partial demo for them. This can be a great chance to gauge their response to your product itself, bring up relevant questions, and better understand any concerns they may have. I would recommend against doing a full product demo, though, especially early in the process. Doing a full demo can have the undesired effect of making your customer believe they understand everything about your product, and it will be much harder for you to create a meaningful Reason to Return for another visit. When executed properly, a partial demo allows you to uncover an abundance of information that can then be followed up at a later time with a powerful demo that addresses their core issues.
- **Industry meetings** - No matter what industry you are selling to, there are always big society meetings that your customers might be interested in. Do the legwork ahead of time to see if there is one coming up that is accessible to you, and if there is, ask if they are planning to attend. If not, offer to go for them and bring back any information they might be interested in or relevant to them. This can be a great way to show them you are here to help them, not just to make a sale.
- **Interesting publications** - A compelling case study, industry blog, or information from a social media group dedicated to your customer's industry can be great ways to initiate a return visit. Offer to come back with a case study you

recently came across that you would love to show them and get their opinion on, and use it as an opportunity to build your understanding of them. Be aware of potential pitfalls with this, though. If you realize through your conversation that this study is one they wouldn't respond to (maybe it is about foreign-made components when they only buy domestic), you will need to be prepared to either alter your plan or set up the information you are going to share and dissociate yourself from it ("I know you only buy American-made tires, and this study focuses on foreign-made, but it still brings up a few points I'd love to hear your opinion on").

A Reason to Return can be anything that is meaningful and interesting, demonstrating to your customer that you are going to bring real value to them every time you come back. The better you do this, the more your customer will trust you, and the more you build that trust, the more willing they will be to explore their emotions with you around what using your product could mean for them. As soon as you lock in a Reason to Return during a sales call, the stress of trying to cover every single point goes away. You know you will have more time to earn their business, so you can relax and just be yourself. You are still in the game, which means you still have a great chance to win.

NOW GOALS

If your sales cycle typically takes three or more interactions, then obviously during the early part of the sales cycle, your number one goal is not to close the deal. Even though it is important to keep that big-picture goal, closing the deal, in mind, your emotional bandwidth and energy should be focused on your next few moves, not your final move. In every interaction with your customer, you should want to influence some micro-level change that leads to your ultimate macro goal: earning their trust and their business. You need to identify your ultimate destination, the place you ultimately want to be with this customer, and work backwards, breaking the journey down into small, specific checkpoints you can meet along the way. This will give you direction even in the challenging moments early in the process, bringing purpose to the pain.

A great way to do this is with a prioritizing process I call NOW goals. NOW stands for "Needs over Wants," which applies to both you (laser-focus on what you *need* to get out of each sales call will keep you going in the right direction) and your customer (working to understand their deepest needs will help you determine how to move forward). NOW goals help you focus on what is most important in the moment, informed by the big picture but not trying to do everything all at once. It helps you stay on track, avoid paralysis by analysis, stop procrastination, and say "no" to things that aren't important to your overall trajectory.

NOW goals will look different for different industries and different for individuals with different lengths of sales cycles. The analogy I used was to think about a rock climber setting a goal to secure their safety line to the very next bolt. Bolts are pre-inserted anchors that allow the climber to attach their carabiner to it and continue on. This assures them that they will not fall past this point while giving them smart achievable accomplishments along the correct path.

NOW goals are like bolts that rock climbers ascend

toward. They look up and identify the next bolt they are trying to reach. Once they've secured their line, their progress is secured; it is like a checkpoint. Even if they do fall after that, they will be safe, and they will be able to start again from there rather than going all the way back to the beginning. Let's say a rock climber wishes to set a new personal record and climb a thousand-foot rock in eight hours to beat their previous time. The most important thing for this climber to do is assess the entire climb and then break it down into important achievable segments. As they start the climb, they might even narrow their focus, concentrating on the immediate terrain, looking for footing or something to grab while working in the direction of the next bolt. Celebrating the achievement of reaching the bolt and using that energy as positive momentum toward the next one. It would not be wise for them to have all their thoughts on beating the clock, continuously staring at the top of the mountain gauging how much further to go, constantly checking their watch, and selecting what seems to be the fastest pathway as they go. Thought processing like this will result in taking what appears to be a shorter route, but missing three or four vital safety bolts on the way, a dangerous way to climb. In the sales world, this is when you find yourselves sending email after email with no reply.

Preventing a great prospect from ghosting you and keeping you relevant with the customer is what NOW goals can do for you. They give you something to focus your eyes on during each individual sales call. If you can accomplish your NOW goals, you will be saving your progress for your next sales call, giving yourself a reliable place to start back in and an anchor that will keep you safe and on track if something doesn't go according to plan in your next interaction. Also, let's be honest: sales individuals love wins. NOW goals will allow you to find wins in every sales call and keep the positive momentum moving forward.

Your most important NOW goal is always going to be creating an interesting Reason to Return. Making sure you give yourself a way to stay in the game, keep your sale alive, and to avoid hearing those dreaded words: "Do not call us; we will call you." It is important to go into each sales call with your NOW goals mapped out in the order you believe is most important to keep the sale alive. The priority of your goals will vary industry to industry, but here are some examples of NOW goals you might consider:

- Securing an interesting and meaningful Reason to Return
- Having the customer *anticipate and look forward* to a call back from me
- Identify a way they will benefit from your product
- Learn how knowledgeable your customer is about your product, service, technology, or industry
- The core issue attached to their largest pain point
- Assess whether they are a good customer for you and whether your product is right for them
- Learn what the perfect purchase would look like for them (e.g. would they consider a fast and painless transaction as perfect; or would they consider the white-glove, red-carpet-pampered experience as perfect and do not care about price; or do they love a good deal and do not care if they have to find their own trailer to get the product home?)

- Learn about possible positive or negative emotions they may have toward previous products they've used (e.g. a bad previous experience with a warranty issue)
- Learn their perceived value of your product—how does the price of your product compare to what they *think* the price should be? Potential obstacles?
- Place a cognitive trigger that makes them think of you when the product they use falls short of their expectations or to avoid "out of sight out of mind" when it comes to reordering time.
- Hear them express a personal need for the solution your product or service can offer (this usually will not happen during the very first sales call)
- Have them become your loudest advocate and a part of your journey

NOW goals are not about time management. They are about priority management. They are about making sure every single sales call has purpose and a clear definition of what success looks like, and setting you up to see the small victories along the road to your ultimate goal.

Discovered by psychologist Bluma Zeigarnik, the "Zeigarnik Effect" is the idea that the human brain remembers incomplete tasks better than completed ones. Essentially, our minds hate unfinished business. As long as you leave a task unfinished, your brain is in an uncomfortable state, consuming your emotional and mental energy.

If your only goal going into a sales call is to make a sale, you are going to be feeling the unpleasant sensation of the Zeigarnik effect quite often. To avoid this, use NOW goals, go into your call with specific goals and a real idea of what success looks like. You will give yourself the opportunity to leave every single sales call with your tasks complete and small wins. Creating achievable measures for success helps your brain feel more successful, and it creates momentum to keep that success going in future interactions with your customer. Positive momentum is real, and using NOW goals will give you that positive momentum as you work toward the bigger victory you are battling for.

NOW goals do more than just help you feel good about yourself, though. They help you prioritize and strategize with the big picture in mind. They form good habits and muscle memory over time, since many of your NOW goals will be similar across different customers. They give you continuous small victories that help you keep going, meaningful mile markers along the way for both you and your customer.

My Grandpa was a POW in World War II in Japan for two and a half years. He was in prison with some of the survivors from the Bataan Death March, and one of them told him that the way he survived was one stick at a time. As he walked, he would choose a small goal for himself five feet ahead, a stick or a rock or a flower, and try to make it there. Then, he would find another, and then another, and then another. My Grandpa, along with his fellow Marines, was captured on the other side of the island, so he didn't make that journey, but he survived his two and a half years in a Japanese lead mine with the same mentality: one task at a time. My Grandpa shared that the ones who had the hardest time and did not survive were the ones who lost touch with their immediate needs and only focused on freedom.

This is a heavy example, much heavier than anything

you will experience on a sales call. However, it speaks to the power of goals that are meaningful and achievable, the power of small victories, and the way intentional incremental steps can lead to a larger overall goal. It is one of the many things I learned from my Grandpa, and sales is just one of the many areas of life that it applies to.

NOW goals are the bridge between the present and the future. A person with no vision of the future will always return to the past, and a person with goals that are too big will find themselves starting from scratch too often. NOW goals will help you stay clear-minded in the present with the future in mind, understanding how each small step leads toward your final destination.

So, use NOW goals. Take them seriously. Set up Meaningful Measurements that will help you focus on them and increase your AQ. Become more aware of how you are doing on meeting your goals for each sales call. Use them well, and they will serve you well.

TRUST THE PROCESS

If I can leave you with one final thought on strategy, it would be this: always value your effort and execution more than your results. We want good results, of course, but some of that is outside of your control. You can not control your customers, and you do not know what extenuating circumstances you may run into, but you can always control your own effort and strategy, the work you put into planning your meeting, and how well you execute it in the moment.

This is why Meaningful Measurements are so important. After a sales call, you shouldn't be measuring your success based on whether the customer said everything you hoped they would say. You should be asking yourself whether you met your NOW goals. You should be praising yourself for your effort, not your results. The same goes for sales managers too—if you want your people to create habits that will lead to sustained success, then don't just celebrate results, praise their effort and proper execution.

Focusing on your own effort and execution will help you create those good habits that will carry you over time. It will help you break out of a slump if you are in one. It will help you see success and enjoy your journey even if you are in a season where the tangible results aren't what you want them to be. Focusing on effort and execution will keep you doing the right things, preparing well, putting in the work, strategizing intentionally to set yourself up for success during each sales call.

CHAPTER 8
ARTICULATE YOUR MESSAGE

I HAVE BEEN IN THOUSANDS OF OFFICES THROUGHOUT MY career, either as a customer, a sales individual, or an employee. (Maybe you have, too.) When I walk into an office that is running extremely efficiently, it's like watching something magical. It's hard to even describe exactly what's happening. It's like the people working there can predict each other's actions and read each other's thoughts. There's very little small talk or, as I like to say, "beating around the bush" when asking a difficult question to one another or instructing a risky action. No one's feelings get hurt, everyone seems to be teammates on a solid team. Efficiency at its best with nobody wasting anyone else's time.

In sales, I have observed something very similar. The reps who can walk right in, wave to the gatekeeper as they walk by, say a quick "Hello" to a few other office employees, walk down the hall toward their customer who appears happy to see them, and start talking business right away. This visiting rep gets the important information out of the way first, then they read the situation and their customer's body language to see if they should continue their visit or finish for the day (after making sure they have a reason to return, of course). Then, on their way out, the rep brings the staff up to speed on the work-related information that they just shared with their boss, along with the return date and the reason for the return so the staff can expect them back. Side note, these informative goodbyes may seem insignificant, but to me they have become a lead indicator whether or not the rep I'm accompanying will close this deal or how strong the wall is keeping the competition out. It allows you to educate the staff and remove negative emotions that usually accompany rep drop-ins. It does not matter what country I'm in when I observe this taking place, the staff and the decision maker welcome a fast-paced exchange of information even if it ends with casual conversation that happens to go against what I am saying by extending the meeting slightly over the allotted time.

The term "first impression" seems to have implications that expand past an initial introduction. Maybe we should adopt the term "early impression" so that we can use it to describe the beginning of every meeting, whether or not it's with strangers, acquaintances, or colleagues. The tone and perception of any meeting is established within the first 30 seconds. As long as that initial perception is one where you're not going to waste everyone's time, then you're welcome to share some additional information or ask a few more questions.

These "early impressions" can accelerate your trajectory. If your introduction comes across forced and cringey, then hold on tight because you're accelerating right into a difficult sales call. On the other hand, if you do just the right amount of online stalking and get lucky with using that intel with just the right ice-breaker, then congratulations! You were able to quickly establish rapport, and now your positive trajectory is about to accelerate. Starting sales calls with personal information is a high-risk game to play. Live by the sword, die by the sword. As a coach I find it more impactful for the sales rep to focus on being themself, find the style and approach that they feel more comfortable with. Let me reiterate this; it's most important to find your style, then learn to pivot off of that foot to fit the environment, situation, or customer's body language. Don't just blindly assume they want you to force small talk into the introduction.

Personally, I tend to skip small talk until I get a read on the customer and see how busy or stressed out they are first. Everyone wants to feel valued, and respecting a busy customer's time is one of the best ways to show them that you value them. Their time is a gift to you, and it is on you to use it respectfully, in a way that brings them real value. Even the employees who report to your customer (the decision-maker), those employees are charged with helping protect their boss's schedule or just want to be able to go home on time. They want to know that you respect their time and are truly bringing their boss something valuable when they allow you in the building. Your predictable behavior will help gain the trust of the people around the decision-maker, which will make it much more likely that they continue to allow you to schedule time with their boss rather than blocking you from scheduling anything with them.

This doesn't mean that you need to be short with your customer or cut them off if they're talking or venting to you about something. If they're venting, let them vent. It's an opportunity for you to listen and learn from them, and it could be that the best way for you to bring value to them that day is to just be a good listener. Just make sure you are not the one consuming all the air space. It is important to be aware of the time you are taking up while you are sharing with them, and to understand that every minute of that time is a valuable asset that they are sharing with you.

So, when you are articulating your message during the first or second sales call, think of it as a synopsis of a movie script. You're giving them more than just a two-sentence tagline. You are not reading the entire script. You want to say enough to clearly communicate what is most important for them to know about your product, but you do not want to say so much that you lose their attention and leave no room for them to ask questions or engage in conversation with you.

Human attention spans are shorter than ever. In this age of instant gratification, social media, and quick scrolling from one thing to the next, there are times when you might be lucky to get fifteen seconds of someone's full attention.

So, make it your goal to move through this step in two minutes or less. This will take intentional planning and disciplined execution, but it can be done. If you do it well, you will find your sales skills immediately improving along with your revenue. The faster you capture their attention in the beginning the easier it is to transition and move on to the most important part of this process, which we will cover in the next chapter: Listen and Learn, where you will learn a lot more if you talk a lot less.

We are going to talk about some specifics in this chapter about how to articulate your message in a way that will connect with your customer. Before we start, I want to note that I didn't just choose the word "Articulate" because my son suggested it as an "A" word for my SALES acronym. I chose it because unlike other similar words like "present," "teach," or "lecture," the definition of articulate means to communicate in a way that the other person will receive and understand. You can do a perfect job presenting or teaching, but your customer could be daydreaming about something else. When you *articulate* your message, you are connecting and sharing information with intentional awareness of the person receiving it.

VALUE THEIR TIME

This might feel counterintuitive, but more times than not, people will appreciate you skipping the small talk and jumping right into your message. Getting right to what you came to share with them is not rude, it is actually a sign that you value their time and respect their busy schedule. If they have time for small talk, you can always do that at the end of your meeting.

If this feels strange or impersonal to you, consider using a light "pre-apology." This is something I did with my existing customers on a regular basis. As I entered my customer's office and made eye contact with them, I'd jump right in with, "Before I forget, I wanted to tell you about something I just learned. . ." Another rep I observed often said, "Hey, I'll be honest, it feels weird to me to jump right into this, but I really want to be respectful of your time, so if you do not mind, I wanted to show you. . ."

The approach that the other rep took was not my style, but it seemed to work just fine and it was truthful. The key is to find something that works for you. It's never a bad thing to be honest and authentic with them. You'll only further emphasize how much you respect them and value their time. As you build this consistency and predictability over time, you will start to notice that people are answering more of your calls and are more open to your last-minute meetings because they know they can count on you being respectful of their time.

I observed some of the best "getting straight down to business" examples with an amazing European rep named David. When he would gather potential customers together for dinner, he would announce right out of the gate: "Let's talk business first. That way we can get it over with and enjoy the rest of our meal, and no one's judgment or memory of commitments will be impaired by cocktails." (That last line often got a laugh.) This was an easy way to jump right into the message David had brought to share, and no one received it as him being cold. They appreciated it, and they understood that it was his way of valuing their time and making sure the meal didn't drag on late because he waited until the end of dinner to present his important information. I have observed over ten of these dinners with David; in various countries and customers, every time the customers value his upfront agenda, respect of time, seat assigning, and especially his honest straightforward delivery style.

Showing your customers that you value their time can be uniquely challenging early in your relationship with them, especially if it is in a cold call. Some people have an easier time cold calling than others, but if you are someone who doesn't like it, there are some great tricks to make it easier to do it in a way that feels authentic to you. For example, when I sold security systems, I often knocked on neighboring doors while I was doing an installation to see if any other businesses were interested in upgrading their security. If they said "no," I'd ask their permission to come back if I heard of a burglary in the area. I would even go as far as sharing that if they'd decide to get a security system with me, then I'd throw in a free camera to help with the rear entrance I'd noticed was a little unprotected. This showed them that I was invested in their best interest, and it gave me a potential Reason to Return.

Every single time you meet with your customer, you need to share something of value with them. This is one of the most crucial parts of this sales process, and it is one of the key elements that separates it from other approaches that are out there. You want to leave time for listening and learning, but bringing them something interesting and meaningful every time you meet gives them something valuable for their time, even if they do not end up purchasing your product or service.

This could take the form of just feeding them lunch. You get their time, they get a meal, but if you strive to be more creative than that, both you and your customer will gain more. Think about how this principle applies outside of sales. In today's world of constant advertising and short attention spans, the only commercials we do not regret watching are the ones that teach us something interesting. On social media, no one ever regrets watching videos that contain interesting, novel life hacks with several cool productivity tips. Imagine your message leaving that type of emotion, and one where the individual wants to share what you taught them by sending you to a peer of theirs, resulting in a referral for you.

Look for opportunities to spark curiosity in the people around your customers, people who may not directly be a part of the decision-making process, but who could be equally impacted by it. You want these people to have a high view of you and your product! When I was selling capital medical equipment, I would sometimes walk through hospitals from department to department rolling my vital sign monitor around. It was turned on in demo mode, and the brightly colored screen helped spark curiosity as I rolled up to each nurses station. As I was in the middle of a conversation with them, I would slip the pulse oximeter on their fingers like a street magician, sharing with them in a live demo how our company had new technology that reduced false readings. This was a great way to spark their curiosity and help them understand the product. Even better, they would often send me to the hidden decision-makers or direct me to another department that might need new monitors.

As we discussed in the previous chapter, the specific content of your message can be relatively flexible, as long as it brings value. It could be a case study, a customer story, a proposed law that will affect their industry, information from a conference, a partial product demo, anything that will be interesting and meaningful to them.

If you can share your message through a story, especially early on, that is a great place to start. Story selling is powerful because change comes easier when people can relate to others who have had similar experiences. It engages their emotions in a positive way.

A good story even affects us biologically. It induces dopamine, which creates more focus, lasting memory, and motivation. It induces oxytocin, which allows us to be more generous and trusting, creating a strong connection. Along with the release of dopamine, an interesting and vivid story can help release endorphins, which allow us to be more creative and relaxed.

When I was selling security systems in the 90s, I would often call people a month or so after selling them a residential security system to see how they were doing and in hopes of getting a referral. In one of these follow-up calls, a customer told me about how much they *loved* their blue light.

For an extra seventy-five dollars, we offered a very bright blue light that could be added to the front porch. I would sell it as an additional safety feature so that if the police or an ambulance were called to your house, they would see your home immediately and not accidentally drive past it (keep in mind, this was before GPS became so ubiquitous). This customer shared with me that their teenage daughter turned on the blue light (without the siren) every time someone knocked on the front door in the evening and she was home alone (both parents worked late, which was why they bought the alarm system in the first place). Even if she had ordered pizza, she would turn it on as a deterrent to anyone who could see it. If the pizza guy ever ran off then there is a chance he was not really the pizza guy, or that he had ill intentions.

I had never heard of anyone using the light like that. I loved the story, and I started sharing it with all potential customers. It would quickly get potential customers to share insight into their situation with me by either telling me what a great idea that was or that they would never need it because their kids are never home alone. Either way, I got to understand my potential customers more, and when the time was right I could offer the solution that fit them best. Sharing that story was a doorway to a meaningful conversation that helped me keep their attention and get them to engage with me.

I experienced the other side of this when I worked for Edward Jones. The most common product we sold at Edward Jones was mutual funds. With so many different funds and mutual fund companies to choose from, it was my job as a financial advisor to help my clients choose wisely. I would research various funds, but I also had mutual fund wholesalers who would cold call me, trying to sell me on why I should offer their mutual funds to my customers. For these mutual funds, I was experiencing both the buying and the selling end of the sales process. I was the customer, then I transitioned to being the sales rep.

When these wholesalers would contact me to schedule a visit, I would always make time for them, even if I had to rearrange my schedule, because I knew they were going to bring value. Every time they visited me, they'd share why it was the right time to invest in a certain sector, accompanied with a great story that I knew I could share with my own customers. They got my attention and won me over, and they equipped me to do the same. I could go to my customers and essentially repeat the same stories they told me. I experienced the power of those stories as a customer, and then I got to turn around and observe their power as I shared them with my customers as a sales rep.

Whatever your message looks like, share it with authenticity. It is good to show confidence in your knowledge and experience, but make sure it is genuine. Projecting false confidence can be a red flag to customers in most situations. Show them that you are willing to listen to them, that you are working to understand what kind of message would be most interesting to them. This will help them trust you more, and as their trust in you increases, their trust in your message will as well.

In the two minutes you spend sharing your message, think about these three goals:

- **Share something meaningful and interesting.** You may not have full awareness of what their biggest pain point is in your first meeting, but do the best you can with whatever information you have. If you have an understanding of what challenges they are facing, make sure your message is relevant to them. Make sure the delivery of this message is not directly targeting their specific situation. You don't want to lose credibility by acting like a know-it-all and then missing their specific pain point. Phrase the information so that it is easy for them to tell you "I would never use that feature." and with that reply you can now learn why.

- **Show how you can help.** Through whatever you share—a story, case study, demo, or anything else, help them understand how your product's features and advantages can benefit them. You want to be a wise guide on their journey, like Alfred to Batman, Yoda to Luke, Mr. Miyagi to Daniel-San, Merlin to Arthur, Morpheus to Neo, or Dumbledore to Harry. You are their consultant to find them a product that fits, not force your product on them.
- **Deliver info in a way that encourages their opinion.** Whatever you share needs to leave room for your customer to ask questions and share their thoughts, and it needs to be interesting and meaningful enough to them that they will share it with others after you leave.

If you can accomplish those three goals in your two minutes of sharing your message, you are setting yourself up for success. At the very least, you will walk away having learned more about your customer, and as long as you set yourself up with a Reason to Return, that is one of the best outcomes you can have.

CAPTURE ATTENTION

You are always competing for your customer's attention, and with so many different sources that want their attention in today's world, working hard to earn it is more important than ever.

Dr. Yearwood, who I mentioned earlier, was very creative and always inventing new procedural ideas. We had a great working dynamic, which led to lots of great conversations and brainstorming sessions where I got to learn about how his brain works and hear some of his great ideas. So, anytime I saw something written in a publication that made me think of him or an idea he had shared, I would want to show it to him. (He was constantly spitting out great ideas, so this actually happened fairly often.)

Instead of emailing it or dropping it off where he might not see it or have time to read it, I would hand-deliver it to him. I wanted to see his body language as he read it, hear the first thoughts that came to his mind as he processed the article, and most importantly learn from him as he read it. Like a kid with a winning raffle ticket, I would come down the operating room corridor waving the paper at him saying, "Dr. Yearwood, someone stole another one of your ideas!" This sparked curiosity for him, which meant I had his full attention. Which in all honesty is the same thing you want from a best friend or a loved one when you see them. It was no different with Dr. Yearwood. I always knew this would lead to a smile and great conversation where I could learn more about this publication and his thoughts about it.

I have seen this work all across the globe. In northern

Germany, I observed the very same strategy from a German rep who happened to be 6 '5 ", not an easy guy to miss. We arrived at the hospital a little earlier than expected, thanks to no traffic on the Audubon. As soon as we got changed into scrubs and entered the OR corridor, the rep held up some paperwork over his head and gave it a light shake in the air. I could see his target, the surgeon at the other end of the hall, and I observed the immediate change in his body language when he saw this giant sales rep holding up a paper for him—he was excited. It was obvious that this rep had built up predictable behavior with this surgeon in a very positive way, and the expectation was that they were about to have an interesting and meaningful conversation. That is exactly what happened. They jumped straight into discussing the paper, so quickly that I didn't even get introduced to the surgeon until after they had talked. This rep was obviously an expert at how to spark his customer's curiosity.

Attention is a blend of curiosity and anxiety. Think about the things you pay attention to in your own life. They are either things that you are interested in and want to learn more about, or they are things that you need to pay attention to because something bad might happen if you do not. In many cases, it's some combination of the two. Let's use your doorbell as an example. If it rings at 11:00 a.m., you will feel mild curiosity and low anxiety. You might wonder what package is being delivered or if it's a solicitor. You will pay a decent amount of attention to the door, but you probably will not give it your full attention. Now if that same doorbell rang at 1:00 a.m., it is safe to say you will have a much higher level of anxiety and probably a higher level of curiosity, which combined would direct 100% of your attention toward that door.

This is the case for your customers as well. If they are facing a problem that your product would help them solve, they are likely facing some level of anxiety around it. There may be a time in the process, after you have gained their trust and built up enough positive feelings, that helping them explore their anxiety could be a genuinely helpful conversation. Similar to the 80/20 rule we talked about earlier surrounding positive and negative emotions, we want to work to gain their attention primarily through sparking their curiosity, not so much their anxiety. If you do this well, it will still spark their interest and lead to meaningful conversations with them. More importantly, it will make them much more likely to want to talk to you again.

If you spend every sales call focusing on everything that could go wrong in their life or career if they do not buy from you, it is not going to make them feel very good, even if everything you share is true. This is the technique used in question-based selling, which we talked about in chapter three. Your customer might recognize their need for the product you are selling, but they probably will not look forward to seeing you again and might even look to buy it from someone else, as soon as you finish convincing them that they need it.

Much like positive and negative emotions, focusing on triggering a person's anxiety is a quicker way of gaining their attention. As with everything in this process, we are not looking for the quickest solution. We are looking for the *best* solution, the one that will truly benefit your customer long-term and create a lasting connection.

Choosing to focus on sparking curiosity will serve you in the long term with your customer. It also means you have to be intentional in the message you choose to share each time you meet with them. If it's your first meeting, share something that you know will spark meaningful, informative conversation, even if you ultimately learn that it is not exactly right for their needs—just make sure to dissociate yourself from it (I will explain later in this chapter). If you have met with them before, use the knowledge you have gained about them to share something you know they will find valuable. This will also help you discover Reasons to Return. In each sales call, you are always working to find something worthwhile to share with your customer in the next sales call.

One interesting and challenging point about attention is the more familiar and comfortable your customer becomes with you, the more they trust you, the more their attention to you will fade. They will feel more relaxed around you, which is obviously a good thing. This can lead to their attention relaxing as well. Think about this in your own life; if you are married, do you pay as much attention to your spouse now as you did when you were dating? If you work with someone for landscaping, pest control, HVAC maintenance, or anything else around your house, do you give them more of your attention now than you did when they started working for you, or do you feel comfortable enough with them now that you do not notice them as much when they are walking around your house unattended?

For me, every time I step into a new operating room, whether it's in Tokyo or in London or anywhere else in the world, I have eyes on me. I specifically have the attention of the circulating nurse, who doesn't know if I even understand O.R. etiquette (the nurse has anxiety—will the new guy accidentally touch the blue sterile tables?). However, as soon as my behavior becomes predictable to them, they immediately feel more comfortable with me. Since they now observed me demonstrating appropriate OR etiquette they now trust that I know my way around an O.R. and like that they drop all their attention toward me.

All of this is ultimately a positive. If your customer is more comfortable with you and trusts you more, it is a good thing. Nonetheless, you have to be aware of how it can cause their attention to wane over time. It is just one more reason why it is so important to search for interesting and meaningful Reasons to Return, things to share with your customer that you know will spark their curiosity and capture their attention. This is how you will continue to spark their curiosity throughout the process, even after they feel comfortable with you.

MAXIMIZE RETENTION

Capturing your customer's attention only matters if they remember the information you share with them. Part of this is making sure that your message is interesting and meaningful to them, which is key to holding their attention in the first place. There are a couple of other key points to remember when it comes to making sure your message sticks with them.

The first is to remember Hermann Ebbinghaus, the creator of the forgetting curve we discussed in chapter five. According to his research, if you share something once, the person you shared it with will only remember 50% of what you told them by the next day. Remember, if you share the same information with them five times over the course of ninety days, that number goes up to 90%.

That means that if you want your customer to retain your messaging, you need to have the big picture in mind from the very beginning. Go into your first sales call with the understanding that you are going to need to make three or four more calls for your information to truly stick with your customer, and choose your messaging accordingly. Focus your approach on foundational learning that your customer can build on in future visits. Do not feel like you need to share every single piece of information you have. This could overwhelm your customer, and it is best to save some to share with your customer in future visits.

Think about the way you are sharing your information with the customer, too. Are you bringing tangible materials that they can read, examine, hold in their own hands? Or are you just talking and expecting them to listen and retain everything you say? People will remember a small amount of what they hear from you. They will remember a small amount of what they see. Now, if you can work the two together, if you can give them a way to see *and* hear your message, their retention increases exponentially. If you do this strategically, you are giving your customer a chance to take in your message twice in the same meeting.

The other key point when it comes to retention is trust. Logically, this makes sense, we are more likely to value information from someone we trust, and we are more likely to remember information we value. When you are actually in the moment, it can be so easy to forget what a key role your connection with your customer plays in their retention of your information.

Thankfully, there are simple, reliable ways to build trust with your customer over time, and this sales process is built around them. Here are a few things to keep in mind as you are engaging with your customer and working to earn their trust:

- **Bring value.** If you bring information that is interesting and meaningful to your customer every time you meet with them, they will begin seeing you as someone who is reliable, consistent, and worth listening to. They will expect you to bring something new when you meet, and they will be ready to listen.

- **Be predictable.** Trust naturally builds with multiple interactions over time, but only if you are demonstrating steady, positive, desired behavior across those interactions. If they feel that they know what to expect from you each time you show up, they will be more likely to trust you and let their guard down to hear what you have to share with them. However, if your behavior is erratic and inconsistent, that trust will never grow. Use AQ and after each sales call ask yourself: how consistent have I behaved in previous sales calls with this customer? How predictable and positive has my behavior been overall? Consider making it a Meaningful Measurement, rate yourself 0—10, and try to grow in your predictability over time.
- **Do not be afraid to repeat yourself.** Repeating the same statistics to your customer might feel redundant, but it is actually worthwhile for two reasons. First, it will help them remember what you are sharing. Second, when people hear the same information multiple times, especially when it comes to stats and numbers, they are more likely to believe it. Some people may abuse this technique (think about certain politicians or cable news networks), but as long as you are approaching your sale with integrity, you can use it for the customer's benefit. They will be more

likely to trust the good information you are sharing with them if they hear it multiple times, and in the process they will be reminded that you are consistent in your messaging, which will help them trust you even more.

BE PREDICTABLE

Predictability in a macro form is a beautiful thing; predictability in a micro form is boring. This next story is not about Dr. Segura, but I need to share details about him to set the stage. Dr. Segura is an extremely gifted physician when it comes to diagnosing pain patients. He has a very successful practice with loyal patients. He is trained and extremely competent in every therapy offered in the specialty of Pain. His outcomes are among the top percentile of his peers. In short, here is a physician who does not need to hear a lecture over lunch in his busy clinic from a pharmaceutical rep or a device rep.

A few years ago, I was in clinic with Dr. Segura collecting some commercial learning data for Spinal Cord Stem (SCS). In the middle of discussing numbers, he turns and says, "You know, Rich is for real. Every time he shows up he brings something new. I mean it, every time I see him he has something new to share! I even changed up my catheter suturing technique because of some best practices that he learned and shared with me. Oh, and all my pump patients are doing great with these new dosing intervals." This is coming from a physician with some of the best hands in medicine. I was taken aback to say the least. Rich Clementi is a retired MMA fighter who got into medical sales after a 15-year successful career in cage fighting. Rich is Dr. Segura's intrathecal pain pump rep and a student of the game, constantly improving his knowledge of pain implants, but when one of the best doctors you know makes a comment like that, it catches your attention.

Rich Clementi is not big on small talk. Even when he was making a living fighting for the UFC and other organizations, he wasn't big on talking. So how over the past 10 years has Rich continuously been one of the top reps, leading his company in sales revenue with no prior sales or medical experience? Easy, Rich never tried to hide the fact that he knows less than the physicians. To him, it was not a weakness; it was the truth. That being said, he was hungry to learn, and he really enjoyed sharing what he learned with those around him. Dr. Segura said, "When you see Rich, get your pen out because you are about to learn something new. You can always count on Rich to show up in surgery with his "A" game, ready to share something he just researched." Both Dr. Segura and Rich Clementi demonstrate the kind of predictable (macro) behavior you want to strive for.

AWARENESS IS KEY

Going in with a good strategy to share your message is huge, but remember: people buy because of what they hear, not because of what you say. That is why it is so important to constantly build your awareness of your customer and how they are engaging with your message so that you can be ready to respond accordingly in the moment.

It is possible that you will go into a sales call with some information to share, but when you share it, you see that your customer is not very impressed. Maybe you are sharing the results of a study that was done on the product you are selling, but they feel that the study had too small of a sample size.

First of all, do not view this as a failure. You've learned something important about your customer, and now you are prepared to shift your approach moving forward. With this new awareness, you can use a technique called **Back Burning** (a term I stole from some real heroes who I went to school with and are now firefighters). This is something firefighters do when they are battling a fire. They actually intentionally burn brush in the opposite direction to make the overall situation safer and easier to handle, removing fuel from the fire's path and allowing them to get out in front of the fire and take control.

It is the same in a sales call. If you want to share some information with your customer but know there is something there that might be an obstacle for them, do not hide from it. Get it out of your way from the beginning and call it out. "Hey, I wanted to show you this information because I really think you'd find it interesting. I know it's a small sample size, not something you'd want to write in stone—but it's still something to pay attention to, and I would love to get your thoughts on it." Or, "Check out this article. I know it's not perfect, and I heard you mention before that the author is an idiot, but you need to see this comparison chart. It's the only part of the article that seems accurate." You are calling out the elephant in the room and still giving yourself a chance to share your information. Doing this will build credibility with your customer and give you the chance to learn more about them.

Another approach to this is called **Dissociation**—offering a story or an idea to your customer without suggesting that you are offering a specific solution for their situation. For example, imagine that you are selling capital equipment. You may say, "I heard that the new lease rate on capital equipment is better than financing it through a lender. I am going to sit down and do the math to see if that is true. Have you heard the same thing?" Interest rates are changing everyday, so it is not a detail you would be expected to know. Also, positioning it this way gives you a chance to find out how your customer feels about leasing without you offering it as a specific solution for them and losing credibility after you find out they hate leases. Dissociation gives you a chance to share information while distancing yourself from the source, or even belief of the information itself, as you continue to understand your customer. It is a perfect approach to use when you are feeling lost with a potential customer and you want to see how they respond to a possible solution without losing credibility if they hate it.

For example, if I am working with a customer who wants to buy a truck, but I am having trouble getting them to open up to me about what they are looking for, 2WD or 4WD, I might share this: "I once had a customer who would only buy four-wheel-drive trucks, even though he didn't go off-road. He said the reason was 4WD trucks had higher resale value compared to 2WD, and he wanted to make sure he was protecting his investment. When he traded in his last truck, he happened to be right, he got better value from his 4WD than he would have for a 2WD. Hopefully, it will be the same for your truck if we can find you something you like." By sharing this story in an open-ended way and not taking a position myself, I am giving my customer a low-stakes opportunity to share their opinion with me, which will help me gather information that will help me serve their needs better.

Another way to approach dissociation is to assign yourself homework—a strategy that I observed frequently while in Japan with the local sales reps. First, you very "lightly" share something with your customer. Here is an example: "I don't know all the details, and I really want to look into it more, but I just heard about this new 'Middleware' software that is supposed to have the appropriate coding and capability to seamlessly help my software communicate with your existing software. If this is true, it could save a ton of time and make sure that none of your stored data is lost." In this scenario, perhaps your customer disagrees with a reply like, "Absolutely not! There is no way that could be true!" You then can respond, "I initially agreed with you, but the more I research it, the more I'm not sure. Either way, I really want to research it more." Next, you can ask them if you can come back and share your findings with them. Then, ask them if you can come back and share your findings with them.

In that short exchange, you have accomplished several things. You shared some information with your customer while distancing yourself from the information itself. You've learned about them by seeing how they reacted to the information. You've gotten their permission to continue talking about the information you shared with them, even if their initial reaction was overwhelmingly negative. In addition to that, by assigning yourself homework, you have given yourself a built-in reason to return and an opportunity to show your customer that you follow through on what you say you are going to do. This technique is a great way to tackle a subject with your customer that you are afraid they might have strong feelings about. Also, it can reduce any anxiety you have over sharing something with your customer that they might not like to hear.

It is also critical to build your awareness around your

customer's level of background knowledge on the product you are selling. This helps you get your approach right in so many different ways. If you know that your customer doesn't know much about the product or the industry you are selling in, you will know that you may need to do some more educating as you share your message and that you should avoid using a lot of industry language and acronyms. On the other hand, if you know they are already an expert, you will be able to speak to them accordingly, making sure they know you respect their knowledge rather than making them feel like you are talking down to them.

There is also the Dunning-Kruger effect, which we discussed briefly in chapter five. This is a cognitive bias that can cause people to believe they have more ability or knowledge in a certain area than they actually do, and it can be a real obstacle to sharing your message. It creates a sort of combination of the two examples I used in the previous paragraph: your customer might need to be taught about your product, but they view themselves as already being enough of an expert that they are not receptive to your teaching.

If you find yourself in this situation, it can be challenging to find a way to educate your customer. One approach you can use is giving them an easy out. Allow them to acknowledge their need for or interest in learning about one area without diminishing their perceived expertise in another. Or, open up the conversation by asking for their help. Ask if you can share new information that you plan on presenting to another customer to get their opinion on it. You are giving them the opportunity to hear it first and learn about something new without looking like they need to hear it. They get to remain the "knowledgeable customer" and save face. This also allows you to hear exactly how they feel about it when they give you constructive criticism. Be sure to fully receive their criticism, because it will not only help you with them but with future clients, too.

Of course, the best way to get around the Dunning-Kruger effect is to avoid it completely. Work hard to build your awareness early in the process of both your customer's *perceived* and *actual* level of expertise, and build your message accordingly. This will help you choose your messaging and your approach intentionally based on what will work best for your customer, setting yourself up for success from the beginning.

Finally, as you work to build awareness of your customer, remember that you are not always going to get it right. You might miss the mark with your messaging. You might share a study written by an author they do not like, or a statistic they do not find all that compelling and you forget to dissociate yourself from it. We are all human, and we all mess up sometimes.

Hear me when I tell you: missing the mark is okay. Think about it like playing darts. Even if you have a lot of experience, your first throw is rarely your best of the night, but as long as you are aware of why you missed, you can adjust. Your next throw will be better, and eventually you will be throwing bullseyes (or at least in the region you intended). Remember, you will never improve unless you pay attention to where the previous throw landed and make the appropriate corrections.

If your first pitch to a customer misses the mark, use it to adjust for next time. Think about it as an opportunity to learn about them, to ask questions, to better understand how to communicate with them in a meaningful way in the future. It gives you a chance to be human, to show them that you are not perfect. If you show a commitment to learning more about them and their needs, it can even be an opportunity to build trust and credibility.

All of this comes back to your awareness of your customer. If you have awareness of them, use it to build a message that will be as meaningful to them as possible. Once you have built your awareness of your customer, you will understand how to communicate, not just your product's advantages on how it could theoretically help someone, but its benefits to them specifically. That benefit is how your product is going to make them the hero. That is the importance of articulating your message: teaching, educating, enlightening, and helping your customer understand how using your product will allow them to make a real difference.

CHAPTER 9
LISTEN AND LEARN

I HAVE GOT SOME REALLY EXCELLENT NEWS FOR YOU TO START off this chapter: the most important step of this sales process is also the simplest. There are no step-by-step methods to learn, no complicated techniques to practice, no systems to memorize. In this step, you have one job: shut up and listen.

The transition from "A" (Articulate Your Message) to "L" (Listen and Learn) is easy. You just shared something interesting and meaningful with your customer, so now all you have to do is ask their thoughts. For example, if you are sharing a case study, you could say, "I like this study, but it left me with a few questions. I am curious if you had any thoughts or questions after taking a look at it."

Then, after you have shared what you are going to share, just shut up and listen. That's it. Just be a good listener and commit to learning about your customer. Do not be tempted to give a quick solution when you hear symptoms. You are listening for core issues. You want to be able to clearly see, identify, and fully understand them and their situation.

This is the most important part of your sales process for so many reasons. It is where you learn about your customer and how you can best help them. It's where you really start to form your connection with them. It's your chance to show them that you are truly in it for their good, to work on building their trust and positive feelings towards you.

People want to feel understood. The more you really, truly want to understand your customer in your heart, the more they will ultimately want to buy from you. We buy from who we like, and this step is where you can start making that happen. If you are genuinely curious to learn about them, listening without you just waiting for your turn to talk, they will feel it. It's the core of forming a connection with them.

Throughout the entire sales process, it's important to stay sincere, genuine, authentic, and empathetic. That's especially true in this step. Selling is about helping, not convincing, and the only way you'll know how to help your customer is by taking the time to listen and understand them.

You have to believe that going "all in" on this portion of the process is vital, so much that it should consume 80-90% of your focus. The good news is that if you have a genuine interest in your customer, it is going to come naturally. When you truly care about understanding someone, listening to them becomes pretty easy.

ALWAYS BE LEARNING

Listening is great on its own. Although there is an extra bit of intentionality you need to incorporate in this step if you are going to succeed. Make sure you are always working to learn about your customer, paying attention to what they say, learning about their needs, and building your understanding of how you can best help them.

Your goal here is to discover their opinion of your product or the information you shared. Keeping that in mind will give your conversation direction. It will guide you to ask genuine questions with pure intentions that will lead you to uncovering more about them, to guide the conversation. So, in short you are learning information that will ultimately help you help them.

Think of yourself as a podcast interviewer, keeping the conversation on track, then moving out of the way to let your interviewee share. Larry King said, "I never learned anything while I was talking." Yet he was also a master of helping guide a conversation, helping the person he was talking to share about things that would be meaningful to them both.

One of the hardest parts of this process is to stop talking after you have asked your question. It sounds simple, but that doesn't make it easy. It can be so easy to fall into the trap of just waiting to speak when a customer is talking, and that is understandable. When you have a deep understanding of your product and a true belief that it could help your customer, it's natural to feel an eagerness to share all of that with them.

Waiting to speak is not listening, and waiting to ask a question is definitely not listening. Early in the sales process, you probably do not know as much about your customer as you think you do. If they throw you a curveball, an answer you didn't expect, you could be thrown off balance if you are just waiting for your turn to talk. However, if your only goal is to listen and learn about them, getting an unexpected answer from your customer is actually a good thing. These surprises are exactly what you're trying to uncover in this part of the process, and hearing them now can lead to more meaningful conversation and (eventually) help your customer arrive at a solution that actually benefits them.

Once you feel like you have learned something meaningful about your customer, take the time to confirm what you have learned by asking verifying questions. These can often start with a phrase like, "So, I hear you saying that…" This is a great chance to make sure you are truly understanding them, and it also shows them that you really care. It demonstrates the authentic empathy you have for them in a way that will help build their trust in you. I had to do this constantly at Edward Jones. As a financial representative, you have to understand your client's goals and, more importantly, their risk threshold. You might think this would be easy to uncover, but you would be surprised. Clients would ask for high growth and medium risk when, after several qualifying questions, you really learn they want low to medium growth and zero to low risk.

One of the things I admire most about Stephen Shockley, the auto sales professional I mentioned in a previous chapter, is the way he values listening to his customers so much that he actually manufactures opportunities to do so. He understands that before you can listen to them, you have to help customers feel comfortable communicating with you. One of his many techniques for this is something he calls "the long way around." If you walk up to Stephen and ask him flat-out, "Do you have this car?", he'll tell you to follow him, but rather than walk you directly to it, he'll zig-zag you through the entire car lot. As he walks you the long way around, he will put his hand on a car, share something about it, then ask your thoughts. For example, he may stop at one car and say, "This is a new color; what do you think?" and then stop at the next car and say, "This model has the best lease rate because it has the highest resale value. Have you ever leased a car?" He creates natural opportunities to help his customers open up without taking the risk of suggesting a specific solution (remember when we discussed Dissociation in the previous chapter?).

Stephen has done this to me multiple times, even recently, when I stopped by to see him and see a new first-year production sports car that just got delivered. He's so smooth about it, even though I know it's coming, I will answer every one of his questions right up until the point when he turns around and laughs at me, and I realize he did it to me again.

Stephen does this because it gives him a real opportunity to listen to his customers so he can serve them better. He knows that his time with a customer is relatively limited, and he knows that if he just walked them right to a car and asked them a question, he might not get an answer. However, by creating space and time for them to talk about their needs and what they are looking for, he can deepen his own understanding of their needs so the car they drive away in is the right one for them.

As you are listening to what your customer is saying, be sure to pay attention to the unspoken information they are giving you as well. Body language is a big part of this step, and learning how to read it can give you useful information about your customer. If they are leaning forward, making eye contact, nodding when you repeat back to them what you have heard them say, that is a good sign that they are engaged. Although there are signs to watch for that could hint that they are checked out of the conversation as well: standing with their hands on their hips, angling their feet towards the door, checking their watch, touching the small of their neck. Signs like these do not mean that your sale is doomed, but they do indicate that something is not hitting quite right for your customer, signaling an opportunity for you to dig in to try to understand why.

Paying attention throughout this step is one of the best chances to raise your AQ. After meeting with a customer, take time to ask yourself questions about how the conversation went. How often did you ask a meaningful question, one that let the customer open up about something they wanted to get off their chest? How did they feel after the call? What factor carried the heaviest weight in their reaction to your product? What non-verbal cues were they giving you that you should be paying attention to? The more awareness you can build of your customer, the better equipped you will be to help them.

FIND THE "WHY"

"He who has a 'why' to live for can bear almost any 'how.'" This quote by 19th-century German philosopher Friedrich Nietzsche has stood the test of time. Each of us has a "why," the reason we do what we do, the thing that motivates us to get up in the morning. This is true of your customers, too. Your job is to find that "why," to figure out "why" *they* would think they should buy from you, not "why" you think they should.

Another great quote is "Be curious, not judgmental." Often mis-attributed to Walt Whitman, the real author is unknown, yet it perfectly describes your job as a sales professional during this stage of the process. You might see that the product your customer is currently using or the company they are currently working with is costing them time, potential income, positive outcomes, or even just happiness in general. If you react judgmentally, drilling home the point of just how bad their situation is, you run the risk of embarrassing your customer. Even if they recognize that you are right, no one likes to feel that way. They may end up switching to a different product, but it probably won't be yours.

Now, if you lead with sincere curiosity about your customer and what drives them to make decisions, they will feel heard, and you will learn so much more. You have to become a detective or better yet a therapist, trying to uncover the important information about your client that will help you understand them and, ultimately, help you help them.

Here are a few things that can be helpful to learn about your customer as you work to discover their "why":

- **What is stealing their happiness?** Who or what is preventing your customer from optimal accomplishment, maximum efficiency, total relaxation, peace, or joy? What keeps them up at night?
- **Who else is influencing their decision-making process?** Again, curiosity is key here. Be hungry to learn about your customer, even if it means learning that they have built up loyalty to your competition. It's better to go in assuming they love your competitor and let them prove you wrong than to start by listing all the reasons your competition is inferior and start a debate because you offended them.
- **What motivated them to choose the product they are currently using?** Understanding what drove them to make their last decision can help

you understand what it will take for them to ultimately buy from you. If you ask about a product they recently bought that you do not sell, they will feel comfortable sharing all sorts of information. You will learn how they felt about price versus quality versus service, and ultimately how they made their decision.

- **Why are they not already using your product?** This is a simple question, but it is important to understand. Maybe they have a specific reason they are loyal to the product or company they are already using. Although in many cases, the reason is that they are just scared of change. They might be sticking with what they have because it's what they know, it's predictable to them even if it's not perfect, and they don't want to run the risk of switching to something worse.

The tricky part about finding the answers to these questions is that, in many cases, your customer will not give you a helpful answer if you just ask them directly. They may guard the truth and give you a false answer, or they may not fully understand their situation and give you a false answer out of ignorance, thinking they are being transparent.

That is why having a therapist mindset is so important. Be present, give them your complete attention, lean in, and listen closely to what they are saying. When you sense your customer starting to share core issues, previous mistakes, or poor buying habits, be curious to learn more. Ask good, sincere questions. Remember that your goal in this step is to help them avoid any embarrassing emotions attached to the information they are sharing. You will hear them share information that either contradicts itself or is grossly incorrect. I will say this again: it's very important to protect them from emotions of embarrassment or defensiveness as they are opening up and sharing this important information. Cast no judgment; this is a safe place as they share past purchases or the reason they are in this predicament.

Try to do everything you can to avoid making assumptions. Behaviors and pain points do not always match up like a china set. Your customer might be experiencing a problem and responding in a way that, to you, doesn't seem congruent. Here is a perfect example: you are selling advertising, and a customer shares that they are cutting the entire marketing budget because revenue is down. As their sales rep you want to ask them, "Did you hear your own words?" Over the years, I have heard some pretty crazy comments. I could literally fill the book with examples like this. All I can say to you is that what may be obvious to us is usually a blindspot for them. How is it that the customer doesn't see it or comprehend what *they* just said? Here is the simple answer—people are complicated, and we all carry biases with us that influence the way we interpret information and influence the decisions we make. Here are a few examples:

- **Anchoring Bias** - Some customers will be loyal to a certain product or sales rep simply because it's the product they were trained on or the one they are comfortable using. They are hesitant to change because they do not like change.
- **Choice Bias** - People often remember their past choices as being better than they actually were. If your customer was the one who decided to purchase the product they are currently using,

they may be hesitant to admit that your product is a better choice than the choice they had previously made.

- **Confirmation Bias** - Your customer may only trust information that supports their beliefs, which makes them less open to information that would lead them to making a change.
- **Ostrich Bias** - To put it bluntly, some customers just want to stick their heads in the sand. This doesn't have to reflect poorly on them. It might be because they are just really busy and do not want to think about having to make a big change in their life or work. It is a hurdle you will have to overcome if you believe your product can make their life better. This is also common for customers that are very involved in their industry and sit on the board of that industry's conventions or societies. They want to be fair to all vendors, so they do not want to see data proving one product is better than another.
- **Overconfidence Bias** - Like a gambler on a hot streak, some customers will overestimate their odds of future success based on success they are currently experiencing. Even if the product they are currently using is inferior to yours, they may believe it's the best choice if their current results are positive.
- **Bandwagon Bias** - Your customer may have chosen your product simply because it's what the majority of people in their industry are using. Going against the flow may feel uncomfortable to them.

As with all the information you learn about your customer, uncovering their biases needs to be a matter of curiosity, not judgment. It may feel tempting to try to convince them that their bias is clouding their judgment. Your goal is always to understand them better, to grow your knowledge about what drives them, and to discover how you can help.

THE HARDEST, MOST IMPORTANT THING

Listen and Learn is the most important step of this sales process. That being said, the most important part of this most important step is, unfortunately, a little more difficult. It's simple, but it's not easy: patience before solution.

Your heart is genuine. You want nothing more than to help your customer, and you believe your product can do that. So, when they bring up a problem they are facing, it's natural to want to jump in and offer a solution right away. You are trying to help them, and convincing them to use your product feels like the quickest, best way to do that.

Convincing them to use your product is not your job. Your job through this process is to bring them to a place where *they* recognize their need for your product. When you are still working to uncover their problems and motivations, they will not be ready to make that leap yet.

That is why patience is so important to this step. Your job is to listen, learn, and truly understand them. If you start throwing out solutions at a customer too early, they may feel like you were not listening to them. You will remind them that you are a sales rep. Even worse, you could be wrong. Your solution might not actually fix their problem because you didn't take the time to listen and truly understand them, and you will lose credibility in their eyes.

(Of course, sales cycles vary, so you will need to apply this appropriately to your sales cycle.)

Imagine that you have been experiencing pain shooting down your right leg, so you go to a doctor. After listening to your symptoms the doctor quickly decides to put you on an ibuprofen regimen and refers you to physical therapy to work on your leg. You follow the doctor's instructions, getting minimal relief. The pain never really goes away, because the issue was never with your leg. The core issue, the root cause was your L4-L5 disc infringing a nerve in your lower back. Now you can't even get minimal relief; your pain is back in full force plus some because it was not treated at the source.

Now imagine if that doctor had taken their time and gone through the proper steps to diagnose your pain correctly before prescribing a solution. It might feel like you have to wait a bit longer to experience relief, but once the solution comes, it actually works. It addresses your pain, and the next time you or a family member have an issue, you can trust that this doctor will help you address the issue at its source.

Showing patience in this phase will reward you tenfold with your customers over the long haul. Just like the tortoise and the hair. If your big-picture goal is to build long-term relationships, multiple sales, recurring referrals, and loyalty, then being patient as you find the right solution is the fastest way to get there.

A brachistochrone curve is used to compare different rates of acceleration. If you are not familiar with this concept, imagine two marbles being rolled down two small ramps at the same time. One ramp is a straight decline at a 45-degree angle between the starting point and the endpoint, representing the shortest possible distance for the marble to travel. The other ramp has a curved shape resembling the edge of a circle, with a steeper drop for the marble at the beginning followed by a more horizontal path to the finish. This represents a longer path for the marble, but gives it a chance to build up momentum at the beginning.

Which path do you think would be faster? Over these short distances, it stands to reason that the shortest distance between two points would also be the fastest, especially because this marble still gets the benefit of gravity, but that is not the case. The marble that has further to go but has more opportunity to gain momentum wins the race, every single time.

Understanding your customer before offering a solution is like the marble on the brachistochrone curve gaining momentum as it overtakes the other marble. Over the years, I have observed reps take the time to understand a customer, and I have observed reps jump on the first buying signal, going for what appears to be the quick close only to be disappointed and outpaced by the more patient rep. What's really interesting is over the years, I have ridden with the same reps, observing them change their approach for the better and witnessing more productive sales calls yielding obvious results in favor of taking time to fully understand their customer. On paper, it may seem like this strategy would take longer, but in practice, once you have a deep understanding of your customer and their core issues, you are like a freight train, there is no stopping you.

As we discussed in chapter three, there can be exceptions to this rule. If you are in a situation with a customer where the conversation stalls out or you feel like you are having a hard time gaining any knowledge as to whether or not you can actually help them—offering a solution through disassociation can actually rekindle your opportunity to learn. Be ready to read their body language, gauge the reception of your solution, and use all of the information you gain to build your understanding of your customer. This is a risk; if you are met with a reaction of disgust from your customer, you could lose some credibility in their eyes, but it's a calculated risk. If you are doing it intentionally, for the specific reason of continuing to learn, the knowledge you gain can be valuable enough to make it worthwhile.

Listen and Learn is the most important step in the process, and important things take time. Go into each sales call with the expectation and hope that this will take up most of your time, and if it does, it means your customer is opening up to you and sharing valuable information about themselves. None of this is easy, and it takes practice, but if you have the desire and discipline enough to commit to this stage of the process, you will reach the finish line quickly once you start rolling.

I want to pause here to offer a quick note specifically to business owners who are reading this book. When you sell your product, you have a level of knowledge, experience, and confidence with your product that none of your sales reps will ever be able to match. You built your company from the ground up, and that brings with it an inherent passion, insight, and credibility that allows you to approach customers differently and offer solutions more quickly than the people on your team can (or should) do. If you offer a solution and you are wrong, it feels different to the customer because they are hearing it from the owner of the company, and you'll be able to recover more quickly because of the confidence you have developed. This isn't the case for your reps, especially younger or newer ones. The way you close a sale is unique to you; understanding and accepting that is crucial to the development of your less-tenured reps. Do not expect them to be just like you, because they can not. Having them shadow you on sales calls might slow down their development and possibly intimidate them. You can best support them in their growth by encouraging them to observe other sales reps on your team as they discover their own style.

ALL ABOUT THE CUSTOMER

Have the mindset that your customer knows something you do not. Because, of course, they do. You may be a total expert on your product, all the advantages it offers, and even how someone in their situation might potentially benefit from it. Nonetheless, you are missing one key piece of information: what would make your product valuable to *them*. To help them discover what is most valuable about your product, you need to discover what is most valuable to them first.

It can be hard to stay humble when your customer says something that is just flat-out wrong, bad information, a false assumption about your product, or anything else that is just plain incorrect. Our natural impulse is to correct them, to help them understand the truth so that bad information doesn't cloud their perception of your product. Usually, this impulse comes from a good place, you truly want to help them grow their understanding of how your product can genuinely help them.

This is your opportunity to approach your customer with humility and make them know you care. Being humble isn't lowering you, it's simply bringing you closer to your customer. Being humble is not a poor reflection on your competence or intelligence as a sales person. Your goal is to connect with them, not make yourself seem smarter or more important than you are.

Understanding them is much more important than correcting them. If your customer says something that is incorrect or untrue, understanding why they have that belief will benefit you much more than trying to convince them otherwise. The last thing you want is to find yourself in a debate with your customer.

A Navy Seal shared with me that when they make landfall or hit the drop zone, they may encounter an obstacle or a situation they didn't expect, even with all of their incredible preparation and strategizing beforehand. When this happens, they have to immediately adjust in the field. They quickly identify two simple things: most likely to succeed course of action, and most likely to die course of action. Which direction is safe, and which one is not? They are not concerned with the fact that they were not expecting this situation; their focus is on how to deal with it.

If you find yourself in a situation where your customer is wrong about something, there are two pathways in front of you as well: Most Likely to Influence, and Most Likely to Debate. If you tell them that they are wrong or you correct them with a straightforward delivery, especially in front of others, they will be more likely to debate you or dislike you. Now, if you take the time to understand why they are mistaken, you will be much more likely to earn their trust and influence them long-term. So be humble and remember, it is more important to find out why they're wrong rather than telling them they're wrong.

It's common knowledge that a dissatisfied customer will proactively tell anyone willing to listen about a bad sales experience. When you dig a little deeper to identify the driving force behind these negatively charged conversations, you usually find a confident representative who, without knowing, engaged in a logical debate with their customer. It happens to the best of us. It happens very frequently and it probably happens without the sales rep knowing it happened.

You have to be extremely sensitive to survive one of these landmines. Especially with information you know is 100% wrong. Like, it's so wrong that the correct information might even be a part of your business's name or on the back of your business card. Be careful. Use grossly inaccurate information stated by the customer as a cognitive trigger to remember this chapter and take a pause—whatever you do, don't quickly and confidently tell them, "No, sir, I am sorry. You are mistaken..." You may think your delivery is perfect and appropriate, but I am telling you it's not. At all costs, you must protect them from embarrassment! Find them an easy out, make them feel as if they're not alone with this common misconception (if it's true), let them hear their own comment out loud, and sometimes you are even better off ignoring the incorrect comment if it's not directly related to the product. If your sales cycle is short, you might want to quickly qualify how important the wrong info is to the consumer then decide how to move forward, still focusing on protecting them from embarrassment.

Imagine that you are selling someone new windows for their house, and they tell you confidently that they read your company doesn't offer triple-pane windows. You are surprised to hear them say this, because they're wrong. So wrong. In fact, you just sold triple-pane windows to a different customer earlier that day. But rather than correcting them, you take this opportunity to learn. "I have heard that before. I am now wondering if we have old information on our website or older sales sheets being circulated. Do you recall where you saw it?" After you find out where they saw this information, you can show them a brochure, product website, or actually demo the product. Depending on the comment and the product, you can even use it as a Reason to Return by asking the same style of questions above but ending it with a light-hearted comment like, "You now have me wondering if you have insider information on my company. Before I confidently tell you we have it, I want to make some calls to confirm no backorders or discontinuations. This will also allow us to schedule a demo where you and your partner can see it in person."

Debates may vary in relevance, intensity, and audience, but when it comes to outcomes, there is one winner and one loser. As the rep, if you find yourself in a debate, you lose either way. If you lose the debate, your customer will see you as incompetent. Win the debate, congratulations, but at what cost? There is a good chance your customer did not enjoy the interaction, which is the exact opposite of how you want them to feel, and you will walk back to your car without having made a sale. Reflect on your personal experience with vendors, sales reps, and repair individuals. Think about a time you made a statement and they quickly corrected you; or even worse, they were misinformed and attempted to correct you with bad info and then continued to draw a line in the sand with their misinformation only to push you further away. This has happened to me so many times with overconfident mechanics, and every time I share my experience with as many people as I can. In short, avoid the debate.

THE RIGHT CUSTOMER

One of the most fundamental things you can learn during this step, hopefully, sooner rather than later, is whether this customer is actually a good customer for you. They're taking up your time, and it's important to determine whether that is time well spent or time you should be devoting to your other customers instead. Do not spread your seed on infertile land. You must choose who you invest your time in wisely, especially if you sell a product that depends on recurring sales.

Imagine that you have sixty customers in a certain territory, but you were suddenly told that you were only allowed to keep three of them. How would you decide what makes a good customer for you? Would it be someone who's easy to deal with? Someone who's logical? Someone who gives you attention, or who's understanding when you make a mistake? Someone who has produced high revenue and has shown great loyalty to you over time? You need to treat your time like money. Where are you going to invest your working capital (you) to make sure you are yielding the best returns possible?

There are many valid answers to this question. It's important to know what *your* answer is. If they are not the right customer for you, chances are you're not the right rep for them, either. You will be serving them better by telling them that this product is not right for them, and then you will be opened up to focus your time on customers who you can truly help. If you realize that it is not a good fit, be transparent right away. Keep in mind you can also upset them with this message, so it needs to be done very tastefully.

If you are able to educate them on a better product for

their needs, explain what the perfect buyer for your product looks like and ask them if they have a friend or family member that fits that description. Go for the referral! If you have shown them that you respect their time by being honest and not trying to force your product onto them, they will be more willing to help you with a referral.

Sometimes when customers aren't happy, it is easy to get intimidated with servicing them and trying to please them. In these situations, it is often best to just cut bait, let them go, and sometimes even fire them. For example, I once sold to a doctor who tried to play medical device vendors against each other. We all got so caught up in competing with each other that we lost sight of whether or not he was the right customer for us or if we were the right implant device for him. He never inquired about outcomes or reliability, and finally, after a few weeks of pricing games, a leader in my organization said, "Maybe we are not the right company for him. If it is alright with you, Travis, I am going to send him an email letting him know he should work with our competition and we will no longer be discounting our product for him." Bobby did exactly that, and it felt great. In addition to looking out for our company, it felt like Bobby was looking after me and valuing my sanity more than revenue. We didn't make money off of him, but realizing this doctor was not the right customer for us was well worth it.

GO-ROUND

To me, the term "go-round" is a beautiful and smart term. It's an aviation term to describe a last-minute decision not to land. All seasoned pilots are prepared and ready to add power, reduce flaps, and radio the tower, "go-round." I believe student pilots can advance immensely when they learn that "go-round" is an important part of their landing strategy and absolutely nothing to be ashamed about, even if their dad makes fun of them afterward. "Son, you're not even lined up; you're going to land us in the parking lot. Son, you're way too low, you're going to kill us, right into those pine trees. Son, I'm telling you, too much power; we're going to bounce off the other end of the runway. More power, more power, you're going to stall us." In this scenario, the plane is obviously not prepared to land, and a well-executed "go-round" is an excellent next step.

Fighter pilots, as confident and competent as they are, they land on aircraft carriers with all intentions that they'll be taking back off and performing a go-round. In fact, they are so prepared to "go-round" that the second their wheels touch the deck of the aircraft carrier they go "full-throttle" in case the tail-hook doesn't catch the landing cable. Just like landing a plane, there is no harm in performing a "go-round."

Hopefully, you have picked up on the main difference between this sales process and other ones that you may have been introduced to. The difference I am alluding to is a sales process accounting for and anticipating the need for follow-up to close the sale. Even if your business is transactional by nature, you still want a follow-up. Do you want recurring sales and referrals from existing customers? The majority of us need multiple interactions with customers to close the sale. Those follow-ups come in all forms—phone calls, emails, text, drop-ins, formal appointments, demos, in-services, and lunches. We need multiple interactions as both the customer and us navigate through the sales cycle. The Authentic S.A.L.E.S process helps you structure the important variable, frequency, into your strategy from the beginning.

Using AQ as you wrap up your sales call, decide if it's time to move forward or circle back on the next visit to further *Articulate* foundational material, or share something new. By applying this process, you are being more intentional with your effort and resources as you qualify the customer's readiness for your product or service. You are in control of the information and the solution. With their best interest at heart, you decide if more information needs to be shared or if they are ready to receive the solution you have for them.

If you are going to do this successfully, though, you have to make sure you have created a Reason to Return. As long as you have a Reason to Return, you are still in the game, and there is no reason to rush forward in this process. You will have the opportunity to come and meet with them again, share new information, and listen and learn even more.

Once you have made it through the first three steps, the "S-A-L" of this sales process, you just start right back at the beginning. Circle back to strategize, taking time to intentionally plan what you want to share with them the next time you talk. Then you will be able to articulate your message well and open up another conversation to listen and learn from them even more. Repeat these three steps until you feel like they have a good understanding of your product or service and how it will make their situation better, then you will be ready to move onto the next step.

Going back to the start of the process may feel like you are moving backward, but I am here to tell you that is not the case. Approaching your customers like this will benefit you (and them) in so many ways. It will help remove buyer's regret and build trust by showing them that you are truly concerned with learning about them and understanding their needs, rather than just rushing them through the process. It will give you time to learn information about them that will help you avoid suggesting a solution that is not right for them. It will allow you the necessary time to make sure that when you do move onto the next step, Explore Emotions, they will actually be ready. While you are efficiently moving forward, you will find, in parallel, many of these customers will start to share referrals before you complete the sale, thanks to them getting a glimpse of your character.

When they are ready, when you feel that they trust you and you have heard them articulate that **they recognize their problem and their need for a change**, then it is time to move to the next step. You have to be honest with yourself about this, because if you move on too early, you will find yourself in a setback reworking through the same steps to regain credibility. Now if you are patient enough to wait until they are truly ready for the next step, you will be ready for a powerful conversation that will help them envision your product making them the hero.

CHAPTER 10
EXPLORE EMOTIONS

In this book's introduction, I shared a story of one of my earliest sales: a curb painting business I had started. I would go through my neighborhood, knocking on the doors of neighbors I knew. Generally, people responded well, agreeing to pay me to paint their house number on their curb.

Through learned behavior, I purposely avoided knocking on one door. There was a woman who had refused everything I had ever tried to sell to her, from my lawn-mowing business to candy bars I was selling for a school fundraiser. I did not want to be denied again, so I decided to just skip her house completely. That proved to be a mistake, at least in her eyes. When she saw the work I was doing around the neighborhood, she tracked me down and told me she was not about to be the only one on the street without her house numbers painted on her curb. It was the first time I observed both negative emotions and a desire to purchase my product in the same interaction. It was the fastest sale I ever made. I believe the only thing I said was "OK." I don't even recall telling her how much I was going to charge.

That was the moment I understood just how big a role emotions play in sales. Emotions are powerful. They have so much weight that they can drive people to make significant changes in their lives and their careers. In the case of this woman in my neighborhood, emotions proved to be such a powerful driver that she bought what I was selling without me even offering it to her. She was experiencing FOMO (fear of missing out), which is one of many negative emotions that can motivate individuals to take action.

With this great power comes, you guessed it, great responsibility. As a sales professional, you are not trying to use your customer's emotions to manipulate them into making a purchase that is not right for them. You are trying to help them grow in their understanding of their own emotions, to see their situation for what it is, and envision how things could be better. You can see that someone or something has stolen their happiness, and it's your job to help make them aware that things could be better and to work together with them to find a solution. That's why this step is called "*Explore* Emotions." You are not trying to convince your customer that they should feel a certain way. Your role is to be a guide, helping them to explore both the positives of making a change and the negatives associated with keeping things the way they are.

If you have gained trust and educated the customer how the product will make their situation better, then there's a really good chance you have already made the sale before you even got to this part. You will find that this sales process is front-loaded. The faster you find and understand their core issue, the less effort will be needed to close the sale. In this case, "Exploring Emotions" will reinforce the sale. It will help them avoid buyer's regret, identify others that they can refer to you, and help them visualize the benefit of fully implementing or using the full functionality of your product. The last thing you want your customer to do is buy a $10,000 home computer and only use it for reading junk emails.

As we discussed at the end of the previous chapter, determining the right time to move onto this step is critical, and it will vary with each customer. This makes knowing your customer more important than ever. Do they trust you and believe that you're here for their good and not just to make a sale? Do they recognize and understand their problem? Are they open to the possibility of change? **This step is to initiate change.** To help them find the motivation needed to make their situation better.

If you realize that you jumped the gun and your customer is not actually ready yet, it is okay to "go-round." Circle back and go through the process—Strategize, Articulate Your Message, and Listen and Learn. Use what you have learned from them to find more meaningful information or a more relatable story that will help bring awareness to them about their situation.

THE WEIGHT OF CHANGE

Change is scary. It carries with it a lot of unknowns, and in most cases, when people are offered change, they default to second-guessing if the grass is greener on the other side. Even if they acknowledge that making a change could improve their situation, there is so much unknown involved with pulling the trigger that they would often rather just stay where they are. Or, to quote my MBA Economics professor Dr. Lee, there needs to be a net positive margin over the current product to overcome the weight of change.

As you can imagine, trust plays a big part in sales. The trust you earn with a customer carries a lot of weight. Trying to make a sale with no established trust is extremely difficult. It is also difficult to make a sale when the only thing you have is trust. Let me share more detail on this second scenario: you have 100% of their trust, you have generated 0% logic to justify the purchase, and there is 0% emotional desire or drive to complete the purchase. Sound familiar? This happens fairly often when selling to friends and family or even upselling loyal customers. Customers need motivation and comfort before they exert the needed energy to make a change. That motivation and energy comes from a blend of **Trust, Logic, and Emotions**. The mixture of these three will vary from individual to individual and industry to industry. As you are listening to your customer, try and understand which one of these three carry more weight.

Remember that the human brain prefers predictable negative consequences over uncertain outcomes. We choose to stay with subscription-based services even though they are more expensive, because we lack the drive to shop around or the desire to call and switch. Even something that is clearly a personal benefit, like accepting a better job offer, can be scary because of the unknown associated with it. It's psychological, and thinking about it in that way will help you better understand your customer and what they're going through in the midst of the sales process.

I was once involved in a blinded survey of physicians that explored what had the biggest influence on their decision of what product to use for a certain procedure. The results showed that their decision was most heavily influenced by randomized, double-blinded, peer-reviewed studies that are performed by physicians and not paid for by the industry selling the product or written by a physician who is a paid consultant by one of the companies. We call this kind of study a unicorn—it's magical, so rare that people may question whether it actually exists.

Aside from the unicorn, the survey explored fourteen other potential influences, and the second most influential factor in these physicians' decisions was their own personal experiences. That means in most cases, there's no better way to influence a change in behavior than to explore your customer's emotions around their own experience. Companies spend millions in marketing and branding, but there is no bigger driver to decision-making than what your customer has experienced themselves.

This is where all the knowledge you have gained from your customer will come into play, everything you have learned as you have gone through the first three steps of this sales process multiple times. Your goal is to use that information to help guide them through this process. If you have a product you truly believe will improve their situation, then working through this step with them will help them to see their situation for what it is and to envision a future where they could be the hero using your product to make things better for themselves and the people around them.

We've talked about the 80/20 rule and the importance of placing higher priority on positive emotions when selling. That is true in this step of the process as well. You want to help your customer explore the positive emotions associated with making a change. That being said, if they're hesitant to move on from the product or service they're currently using even though it's letting them down, this is the moment to help them see their situation for what it is, and sometimes that can mean exploring the negative emotions associated with it. The best way to influence a change in behavior from somebody is to get them to feel the pain or visualize future pain attached to their present way of operating.

Your goal in this step is to raise your customer's awareness, to help them grow their own AQ of their situation. This can be easier said than done, because we tend to repress pain, especially when it deals with our vocation and is derived from a decision we made ourselves. To ensure your success in this step, make sure your focus is on them and helping them get a good sense of the situation. Do not let "getting the sale" consume your thoughts. Your delivery needs to be authentic and empathetic. It's common for strong and successful customers to inadvertently desensitize themselves to pain. This means they have dulled their own pain awareness attached to a certain product or service they are using. So, if you have a customer like this, just make sure you lock in a Reason to Return.

More times than not, they're just used to the way things are, which makes it harder for them to recognize there's a problem that needs fixing. If I'm farming and my tractor starts seven out of ten times when I hold the throttle quarter open and wiggle the key as I turn it, I will probably get used to it and view it as acceptable. So, if you try to sell me a new tractor, I will not even recognize that I have any need for it. I see my situation as being just fine. The burden is on you to raise my awareness that what I am dealing with *shouldn't* be acceptable, that things could be better, and I shouldn't settle for just "okay."

The same is true in other industries as well. There are medical devices that have an "acceptable" rate of breakage or infection. It is the rep's responsibility to bring awareness to the physician that those rates shouldn't be acceptable and that outcomes could be better for them and their patients. It's natural for anyone to just default to sticking with the product they're accustomed to, even if something much better is available.

When explaining straightforwardly to a customer why their situation should not be deemed acceptable, it may initially appear effective to simply explain the rationale behind it in order to educate them about the negative aspects of the current circumstances. Nevertheless, it is crucial to recognize the potential pitfalls that can arise from this approach. Engaging in such a direct explanation runs the risk of triggering defensiveness, embarrassment, or feelings of shame for the customer. Secondly, you may realize (when it's too late) that they themselves chose the product they are currently utilizing. Consequently, any attack on the product may inadvertently be perceived as an attack on their intelligence or even their character. For instance, if they are a doctor, it might seem as though you are suggesting they are jeopardizing their patients with their decision. If the trust between you and the customer is not strong enough yet, then the customer might feel like you are trying to emotionally manipulate them into buying your product, resulting in a complete shutdown of communication.

The farmer above with the tractor is another great example. Speak a little too bluntly about his tractor and he might want to just prove you wrong out of spite. Thus, feeling defensive or embarrassed by your remarks, he'll be driven to get online at www.brokentractor.com, purchasing a new fuel pump, glow plugs, and hydraulic seal kit for a cost far less than a single monthly installment on a new tractor.

Then for the next month he will be waiting for you to stop by so he can smile and show off his repairs. He might even use your own words against you, "Runs like new, not bad for a fixer-upper, wouldn't you agree?" Like I shared in an earlier chapter, you might convince him to improve his situation, but if handled wrong, it'll be with someone else.

Think of yourself as the protective wise guide during this process. You are with them, by their side all the way through, but they're ultimately the one who is doing the exploring. In some ways, it's similar to how a therapist operates. Therapists could tell their clients right away that they need to just stop an obvious destructive behavior they're engaging in, but it has been clinically proven that a direct approach does not yield as good results. Instead, therapists listen and ask questions ("What do you think causes that…? How does that make you feel when…? What do you think prevents you from…? What might happen if you continue to…?") exploring emotions and leading their client on a journey toward self-realization. The best way to help someone recognize their need for change is to help them see it for themselves.

THE PROBLEM WITH MEMORY

Unfortunately, at times, you will have to apply this process from the opposite side as well; the hunter will become the hunted. Thanks to your competition, if you're in a business with recurring sales and your customer base is growing, it's inevitable that you'll find yourself here or there working harder to retain a customer than you did to earn their business in the first place. This is not a matter of "if" but "when" the competition will try and go after even your most loyal customers. It can happen even if you have been providing them excellent service for a long time. It really hurts when you know for certain that the best thing for them is to remain with you, and switching to your competition will make their situation worse.

The reality is that human memory can sometimes be short or fuzzy when it comes to certain details. Any of us can be drawn toward the shiny new thing, even if everything about our current situation is great. So, it's your responsibility as a sales professional to continuously bring value along with helping your customer remember why they chose you and your product in the first place. You can do this through proactively and intentionally re-visiting the same positive or negative emotions that got them to switch to you in the beginning. Share meaningful stories, best practices, or industry knowledge that continues to help the core issue that you originally solved with your product. Or, you can address new issues by teaching them about the underutilized features of your product, maybe offering a discounted upsell or an additional in-depth in-service to reteach features, letting them feel and see the benefits. This will prevent you from inadvertently taking for granted your customer's loyalty and especially missing out on referrals they would have potentially given you.

An example of customers not remembering "all that you have done for them" happened to Copart, a very large salvage auto auction company. I have an interesting perspective on this company, possibly the only one with three different points of view. I was a consumer of theirs in college buying wrecked motorcycles through their auction. I loved their website, inventory selection, title process, service, and overall infrastructure. Second viewpoint, I was an investor in their stock, owning public shares and recommending them to clients when I was a Stock Broker (best long-term stock I ever put clients in). My third viewpoint, I was an indirect customer when my car flooded and was quickly picked up by them in the midst of all the post-flood chaos.

They're a silent hero. See, if you wreck your car and it is totaled, chances are Copart will pick it up, auction it off, handle the title exchange, deliver the car to the new owner, and wire the auction money to the insurance company. In this scenario, the insurance company is their customer, and one of their many goals is to get them as much money as possible, as fast as they can, helping the insurance company offset the money they initially gave you for your totaled car. Copart is a solid company with hundreds of locations, amazing customer service, incredible logistical capability, first-class trucks, and an enormous network of buyers that allows them to get as much money as possible during the auction to help their customers. In my situation above, Copart auctioned my car off for almost as much I got from the insurance company, minimizing the insurance company's loss. That was years ago, but if you listen to their recent analyst calls, it is obvious that they are still putting their customers first with all their commitments.

During Hurricane Katrina, Copart did an excellent job taking care of their customers along the Gulf Coast. They picked up the flooded cars quickly and recaptured as much money as possible for the insurance companies. They were by far the best option then and still are today.

As the years passed and the emotions from Katrina faded, other salvage auction companies who failed to deliver during Katrina's aftermath, slowly started to solicit the insurance companies who were customers of Copart and tried to win their business with a berate of attention and false promises. Copart was the only company in their industry to come through in that crazy time of need. Nonetheless, a few of their smaller customers were being drawn away with misleading financial projections and overstated promises. All this is extremely obvious for the reps, but difficult to prove until the next natural disaster hits. At which point it would be inappropriate to say, "I told you so!"

So what do you do when you care for your customer and know they're being misled or lied to? How do you remind the insurance companies? How do you share the truth with them or get them to see this logically without coming across as confrontational or worse, sounding like you are begging them to stay with you?

It might seem like a rational plan to just meet with these past customers and logically tell them the following: 1) These smaller salvage auctions do not have enough buyers to get them as much money per vehicle as Copart can. 2) Explain how they will not receive their money as quickly. 3) Tell them that these smaller auction companies do not even own their own trucks, so there's no way they can pick up the vehicles in a timely manner. 4) They'll waste more time on the phone tracking down cars and lose transparency because these smaller auctions do not have encrypted website portals to see where their cars are. Or have transparency on how much money Copart was able to recapture from the sale. If consumers only made decisions based on logic, this plan and type of communication would work perfectly, but we are human, and that is not how we make decisions.

First of all, to save your business you need a Reason to Return that is more interesting and meaningful than just you showing up and begging for business back. Second, you may share a few benefits that might resonate with them, but the benefits you identified might be solving a problem of theirs that only equates to a pain level of 3 out of 10 for them. What you really need to do is uncover the negative emotion that drove them away from you or the positive emotion that lured them away to the new vendor. Then, like in every interaction, make sure you lock in a Reason to Return so you can continue to bring value and educate them on features and advantages closest to their core issue. Be patient as you learn even more about their situation. Then, when the time is appropriate, deliver your solution with an accurate visualization of them achieving their core desires in their specific situation. If you have gained enough trust back, you may even decide to add 20% negative emotion by helping them envision the path they're on that's leading them toward a core fear using past experiences like Katrina but painted in a future context. Make sure your stories and scenarios need to have them as the hero for making the right decision, not you as the hero or even your service/product as the hero. It has to be them because, in reality, it is them; they're the ones in control and ultimately responsible.

Selling to a loyal customer that you're losing, may feel different than selling to a new prospect, but your actions need to be similar; you need to help them visualize a future scenario where they're the benefactor and the hero. You never "tell" them, you "show" them, you visualize it for them, you paint the picture. This is where sales reps screw up; they "tell" the customers how great things are and how worse they will become if they use the competition. These reps don't fully listen; their first instinct tends to be to "explain" rather than uncover what negative emotions are initiating the change in behavior away from their product or what positive emotions are luring them toward the competition. I have observed reps ask "why?" then follow it up with more "telling." It's as if the question "Why?" was really an expression of the rep's pain or frustration, not an attempt to understand. If you're in a situation like this and you're able to find the core issue, then the only way to save your relationship is in the delivery of your message. What you want to share needs to be delivered in a manner that connects with your customer and helps them visualize the correct solution. You have to be cautious on delivering the benefits of your product to your customer, same goes for a new customer.

Let's say you do a great job learning about a new customer and earning their trust. Your new customer is starting to open up to you. This is exciting. They start to share complaints about the old product or company. Then they say the mother of all phrases, the phrase all solution-oriented sales reps love to hear from a new customer, the moment of truth, truth about the issues with their current product. It goes something like this, "I swear, every time I go to use it, it won't…." If you have a heartbeat, you're itching to share the solution! They clearly stated a problem that you have the solution for. Well, you might not want to hear this part, but I urge you to pump the breaks. It may sound like they have full awareness and want to change immediately. I am sorry to be a bearer of bad news; they are not ready for your solution or change. They're just venting like all humans do, similar to you when you're around someone you feel comfortable with. You are gaining their trust. Do not ruin the moment with your solution.

Just like when our loved ones share something frustrating about a coworker, friend, or store clerk, the last thing they want to hear is a solution from you. I know it sounds crazy, but it's true. If you don't believe me, try it.

Start offering solutions the second a loved one tells you how their friend or coworker upset them or betrayed them. Watch how your loved one stops talking and their body language changes. This goes for all humans and especially your customers. You will force them to stop sharing intimate and important information the second you start to inject your solution into the conversation. When in reality this is the most critical moment where you need to shut up and listen. They're ready to share with you. With a couple of genuine and empathetic questions, you will allow them to share very important core issues like serious fears they may have in their present situation or grand desires they want to achieve.

REVISITING

There are few better feelings than when you have a breakthrough with someone, and they start to open up, sharing information they wouldn't share with you before, all because you have finally earned their trust or they are being brutally honest. If it's the first time, then this is an honor. Either way, you should treat it as such. It can range from complaining about their present product to sharing their vision and lofty ambitions that are being hindered by their present situation. The exciting part is that most of these issues and complaints can be solved with your product. Like I shared above, you will most likely be itching to tell them the obvious fix—do not. You might even feel like they are teeing up the introduction of your amazing solution—they're not. If your manager happens to be with you, he or she might kick you under the table as a cue to mention your product or offer the solution. The temptation to be the hero is real in these situations. I'm here to tell you the real power is in your patience to let them finish being heard. They will never receive your solution until they feel heard, and in some cases, not until they self-process what they just said out loud.

Try to visualize yourself in this next scenario. Let's say you work for a reputable company, selling concrete sensors, and construction supplies. After months of hard work, you're now one of the approved vendors for a five-story concrete parking garage. You are selling all sorts of concrete fasteners and anchors to the three decision-makers, Foreman, Controler, and Engineer. After a few demos and an in-service, you have learned a ton about this job and what each decision-maker cares about, and how they communicate. The Foreman is constantly mentioning how they're behind schedule. The Controller sounds like a broken record, reminding the Foreman how much they're over budget and that the sporadic overtime doesn't help. The Engineer is quiet and does most of his communication with a pen. He demonstrates thick skin as he only signs off on things that will ensure the job is done correctly.

Through good preparation, you are excited about your next Reason to Return. You're going to share a possible solution that all three should equally be excited about, even with their individual concerns. A solution that will safely get this twenty-million-dollar project back on schedule and possibly back on budget.

Today, you're going to articulate and demo submersible concrete sensors. These sensors give the Engineer and Foreman more accurate data from inside the concrete. This data is processed through a complex algorithm and gives a qualitative progress indicator, so the Engineer can then notify the third-party concrete test lab to apply their pressure test. The third-party lab continuously receives concrete samples from the job site. They get samples from each pour and then test them a few days after the pour to make sure they're fully cured. This makes it safe to pour the next layer of concrete or operate heavy equipment on recently poured concrete.

Conversation during the Sales Call:

Foreman - This could definitely help us stay on schedule, maybe even make up lost time.
Engineer - It's interesting how I'm the only one not bonused on speed. We are absolutely not changing the way we do it. We will only make our next structural pour when the lab gives us a green light saying that the samples withstand the correct pressure.
Foreman - That's B.S.; you know you're the one telling the lab when to test. What's wrong with you getting a little help with measurements from the actual concrete itself? No one is going to die with you asking the lab to test the concrete a day early. Especially if the sensors show good data from our job site.
Engineer - Well, have you thought about thanking me for keeping your men safe? It's obvious you never had to tell a family they lost a loved one. I have, and that's why we will not change (he grabs the rest of his lunch that you furnished and walks out of the meeting room).
Controller - I was going to ask how much the sensors cost, but it doesn't look like I need to now.
Foreman - Sorry, looks like we're not going to buy your sensors. I don't see the problem, I thought he would've been excited to use them.

You obviously know that didn't go as planned. Actually,

it went horribly, so on the way out, you want to stop by the Engineer's office and fix what just happened. You don't know how, but you want to salvage the meeting. Maybe let him know that he misunderstood your intentions. A part of you so badly wants to tell him your number one concern is safety, that every sales rep in the world cares about safety, that no rep wants to see anyone get hurt because of their product. You want to tell him that his thoughts about the product could not be further from the truth. This sensor can prevent what he said from happening. More accurate data helps everyone make safer and more informed decisions.

This is the moment of truth: offer your solution and clarify your intentions or understand more about what he just shared.

- **Choice A -** Stop by his office, look him in the eyes and let him know that you heard him loud and clear, and understand what he said. Following up with a thank you for sharing the incident that happened in the past. In this moment, if done sincerely, you can honor his lost colleague by asking their name. If done from a genuine place, ask how it happened. Allow him to take the conversation where he wants, even if it's "anti" your product.
- **Choice B** - Or do you tell him, "I want the same thing as you. Use these sensors and see how they help you keep the worksite safe"? Maybe continue on about how you have seen other engineers use them to make sure no one gets hurt. You try to tastefully set the record straight and assure him you care about safety.

The correct choice is "A." do not offer your solution. Make a conscious decision to stop explaining, and get into a receiving mindset. Try to figure out what just happened, understand more about them, and this particular core issue that started to surface. When it's time for you to leave, thank them for their time, and secure a Reason to Return so you can "Revisit" the unaddressed issue on the next visit.

Keep in mind before you leave, you might even hear some comments from the Engineer like:

- It's not your fault; you're just trying to sell a product.
- I'm just tired of everyone else's poor planning becoming my fault when I stop them from cutting corners.
- In the future, when it comes to products like this, you only show me; do you understand?
- I don't appreciate you selling any tools that help them cut corners.

It will take everything in you to not defend yourself. All you need to do is make sure you get an opportunity to see them again. Anything you say in this moment will most likely not be remembered or received. In fact, it will be misheard and mistaken for defensiveness.

On your return visit, the Engineer is acting normal, maybe even more polite than normal. It seems like he might feel bad for your last interaction. Letting him have a week to process is already showing to be advantageous. With his defensiveness gone, you feel comfortable starting the conversation with, "I have not stopped thinking about everything you shared and how important it is to have an engineer on-site. Last week when we were together, I wanted to clarify my intentions during the demo, but I didn't think it was appropriate. I never wanted my sensors to replace the third-party testing lab. I only wanted them to give you accurate data so you can call the lab maybe a little earlier to pressure test the samples. Since the demo last week, I have spoken to one of our engineers to better understand the sensors' reliability and capability. After learning more about their accuracy, I think you might have fun challenging their readings while using them in safe non-weight-bearing pours." At this point, definitely shut up and listen to see how they respond.

If he's on the same page with you, then continue with, "Hopefully, the sensors gain your confidence, and their readings just re-confirm what you already know. I can picture you in a few months not being second-guessed when you tell your concrete Foreman you are delaying the next pour because you say so, the sensors say so, and the lab says so. With us heading into winter, I'm also hoping there is a chance you start to trust the sensors and you look like a hero when you call the lab and ask them to pressure test a sample 10 to 20 hours earlier than normal. Still using the lab as the safety net to make sure no one gets hurt."

Even though these sensors are the right solution for the engineer (he can blame the delay on the sensors), he was absolutely not going to receive that message on the first demo. It seems like every other sales call I am a part of, the customer shares an issue or an emotion attached to something we can solve on the spot with our solution. On these sales calls, I am with other reps, so I have the luxury to evaluate the situation. I ask myself, "If we share the solution right now, will they fully hear it, or are they not ready and need to get something off their chest first?" It's usually obvious they don't need a Hero; they need to be heard.

When a customer opens up to you with a problem, it may feel like a missed opportunity if you do not hurry up and hit them with the solution, but that is not the case. As long as you are creating interesting meaningful Reasons to Return in each of those early conversations, you do not have to rush (assuming your sales cycle is one where you will be meeting with them multiple times). You can "Revisit" the issue later, but for now, focus on listening and showing empathy in the moment, which will help build trust and show your customer that you care about more than just making a sale. Plus, if you pull the trigger on every opportunity that you see right in the moment, there's a very high chance your customer will shut down and stop sharing these failures. Let them vent and get it off their chest. Ask sincere and genuine questions about the issue and help them heal as they hear their own words out loud. Nobody likes a know-it-all that keeps offering solutions.

As I mentioned earlier, when the time is right, you can Explore Emotions, so "Revisiting" the most meaningful issue that you uncovered can be your intro into Exploring Emotions. Throughout the whole sales process, you are searching for their core issue. You do not want to try and solve a problem that only has a pain level of 3 out of 10. You want to find their most important and meaningful problem to solve. That is what makes "Revisiting" so impactful; you can qualify the issue, ask sincere questions, and make mental notes, thinking about a solution but not offering one. After a few sales calls, you might have uncovered five potential issues, and now you can apply AQ, to assess their severity, and "Revisit" the one problem that your customer will benefit the most from solving.

"Revisiting" is a two-part process. First, you are giving yourself a reminder to revisit this issue while they speak freely and get it off their chest uninterrupted. Second, you are returning to share empathy and thoughts on the issue. You are honoring them by letting them know that you've been thinking of them and their situation. You are gaining credit and earning more trust by discussing a solid and realistic solution, one you had time to process and get additional input on. As long as your sales cycle allows time for this approach, you will always yield better results. Try it immediately with loved ones. Listen to them, process what they say, then "Revisit" what they shared with you. You can come back to them in as little as two hours and still see a dramatic difference in how they receive your solution compared to interrupting them with a solution on the spot.

Your job is to make sure the balance of good emotions heavily outweighs the negative ones. The deadliest of those negative emotions are embarrassment and defensiveness. You have to protect your customer from those emotions at all costs. "Revisiting" is by far the easiest and best way to avoid those emotions while continuing to gain clarity on your customer's core issue. I have hosted workshops focusing solely on this concept, so I highly recommend taking notes and using it on the very next person you want to help. This is one you can definitely practice during real sales calls.

In use, this part of the conversation can be really simple; it's just being authentic and thought-provoking, staying curious, continuing to ask good questions, and desire to grow your awareness of your customer's situation as you help them grow theirs as well. Remember, you're asking questions to guide them on this journey, but they need to be the one who does the exploring. You can't tell them how to feel, but you can help guide them to uncover it for themselves.

The specifics will vary based on what you are selling, but it might sound something like this:

You: "You said something in our conversations last week that made me curious. I didn't want to say anything when you first mentioned it, because it's not my product and I didn't want you to think that I was saying something negative about the other company. You mentioned that you had an issue with your equipment being down recently. How many days was it down for?"
Potential Customer: "Almost two weeks."
You: "I'm so sorry to hear that. I feel bad even asking, but how much did that cost your team in lost revenue?"
Potential Customer: "Over ten thousand dollars at least, and then parts and labor to fix it was another five thousand. Altogether, it was about half of what it would have cost to buy a new one from your competition or a third of what yours costs." (A light-hearted jab at your more expensive product).
You: "We are more expensive than our competitor, but not as much as you think. Did the repair company mention whether they think their repair is a band-aid or if it should be trouble-free for a while?"
Potential Customer: "Oh, he tried to upsell us on several other components that he said need to be replaced. Before you even say it, I know your parts are free for ten years and you have loaners to get us back up and running in 24—48 hours."
You: "I swear I was not going to mention the free parts. I was probably going to allude to the loaner, since it would keep you from losing more than two days of revenue. I want to help. I know that buying new capital equipment is always painful, and I don't want to make light of the lost

revenue. But can you imagine yourself five years from now, sitting right here in your office preparing a bid proposal for a new customer, and all of a sudden, your competition calls you and asks if you can handle an order for 2,000 units because their equipment went down, and they don't have access to a loaner because they are not a customer of mine? You kindly say "yes," but you include a 35% additional margin because 50% would be too much. Not only is your 5-year-old equipment that you bought from me still running with no issues, but it has the additional capacity to handle all your needs along with their 2,000 units. You hang up the phone and tell your two partners the good news. Your partners call you a hero and apologize for ever questioning you for buying the equipment with the best warranty and capacity. One of them even gives you back the parking spot he stole."

If you are having a conversation like this with your customer, there is a chance you have reached a true inflection point in this process. A different version of the 80/20 rule comes into play here. The 80% is what you have already done: sharing, listening, teaching, learning about their biases and challenges, understanding their pain point, and building your connection with them. The last 20% is the one final nudge you are going to help them with, exploring their emotions connected to their pain point, so they'll be motivated to make a meaningful change with no regrets. Your goal is not to manipulate them but to help them see their situation clearly so they'll understand what you know to be true: that making this change is truly for their good.

WISE GUIDE

As I referenced earlier, just like in epic comeback stories, the hero needs a wise guide to help them with an energetic montage as they introduce something new to their arsenal and rise to their full potential. These wise guides also bring awareness and enlighten the protagonist on their blindspots. With that in mind, think about how many customers you know that don't end up using a product to its full potential. Let me offer a paradigm shift and reflect on this same scenario but with us as the consumer. How many times have we purchased an expensive product where six months down the road we learn about a feature or benefit we never utilized? This happens for several reasons; our sales rep stops enlightening us the second we say, "I'll take it." Another reason might be as simple as the rep not caring to follow up with us. Let's give the sales rep the benefit of the doubt and say they wanted to, but they didn't give themself a comfortable Reason to Return. This would be where a rep has all intentions of following up, but when they go to pick up their phone and call they don't know what to say, along with no accountability forcing them to call us, so they don't.

If you take this process to heart, you will find your deals starting to close before you ask for the order. Although this is a great feeling, please remember your job is far from complete. Just getting a customer to say, "Where do I sign?" is not the finish line. You want to over-deliver on every promise you made. You want that tailored benefit you shared with them about their specific situation to come true. You want them to be a walking commercial for your product. You need their friends and co-workers to stop them and ask what, how, where, or who hooked you up with that.

OVERSELLING

Overselling is a term that describes a sales rep's actions as they continue to talk about features and advantages while the customer is demonstrating obvious buying signals. Basically, the rep is not listening and is literally talking the customer out of the purchase. Customers start to realize the rep doesn't fully understand them if the rep is still trying to sell them. They don't feel heard, and depending on the industry, this can be detrimental. In some situations, customers will cut the rep off and say, "I'll take it" with an influx in their voice, as if they really want to say, "Shut up and take my money already." Here are some buying signals:

- How fast can you start the install?
- When will the first payment be due?
- I can't wait to show this to Collard; he is going to be so jealous!
- Will you need any other documentation to get the process started?

The real difference between "Overselling" and "Exploring Emotions" comes down to awareness and focusing on the real benefit, not endlessly listing features. When you oversell, you keep talking past the sale, not listening to what the customer is practically shouting at you. In contrast, "Exploring Emotions" focuses on articulating how the product's advantages genuinely improve the customer's situation. You've got to catch those buying signals and acknowledge them, letting the customer know you understand and are there for them. This isn't just chit-chat; it's meaningful communication. By demonstrating awareness and acknowledging the customer's signals, you move from just pushing a product to genuinely connecting with the person in front of you. You can do this by showing interest in knowing their experience once they've tried your product, planting a seed for a future conversation and touch-points that will extend past this transaction.

Now for the “why.” Why should you continue to "Explore Emotions" when your customer has clearly expressed that they are ready to buy whatever you're selling? There are a few reasons. The first is to reduce the buyer's regret and the possibility of the customer returning the product or canceling the contract because they don't fully understand the impact of the purchase. Second, you want them to utilize the product to its fullest. You wouldn't want them to purchase a security system and not activate it, or to pay for anti-virus software and leave it dormant while opening .exe files from a prince named Sterling claiming he needs help securing his inheritance. You want all the women to joyfully wear the jewelry you sold them, feeling beautiful whenever they do. Thirdly, referrals are crucial. You want and need them. If you treat generating referrals as important as achieving bonuses, you'll absolutely crush sales targets! Aiming for referrals indicates that you're providing excellent customer care, which will likely double your income over time.

I'm going to back up for a second and talk about actions to help avoid “Overselling.” Start with understanding the importance of AQ and data collection. You need to be watching body language and listening intently for tone changes, potential resistance, and buying cues. To identify a change, you first need to establish a baseline; this is the collection and mental note of everything going on. Start forcing yourself to watch the customer's behaviors when they are sharing information that has no emotion attached. Watch them talk to others, then see if the same tone and body language carries back over to you. I mentioned early in the book the action that the best reps around the world execute regularly—securing interesting and meaningful Reasons to Return. Now, I want to share the "skillset" the best reps around the world possess—keen awareness and a high AQ.

International ride-alongs, in countries where I don't speak the language, force me to lean on this skillset where I am constantly reading the body language of the customer and mentee sales rep. High-level AQ is obvious to spot in a top-tier rep. They constantly stay one step ahead of the customer. When they get thrown a curveball, no problem. They may not have known what was coming, but they picked up on a slight change in behavior and were prepared for the worst. It's usually never as bad as the scenario their imagination raced to, so when they do hear it, there is a slight reduction in anxiety. Then they call an audible and never skip a beat. The flip side of this is getting completely caught off guard followed by awkward behavior from both you and the customer.

CHAPTER 11
SOLIDIFY

CLOSING IS TRULY AN ART, PERFECTED BY PRACTICE AND repetition. While closing techniques are important, especially within certain industries, I'm here to tell you that they're not the most important part of this sales process. The work you put in before you ever get to closing—connecting, building trust, listening and learning, showing your customer that you are here to help them—is the foundation of the process and is more important than any closing techniques you might use.

Securing a commitment from your customer is obviously important, but you didn't come this far in the process to get them to say "yes" and then just stop caring about them altogether. You've been genuine up to this point, and you need to stay genuine all the way through. Especially as your sale nears the finish line, continuing to understand your customer's needs and how you can help them is the most important thing you can do.

When you are solidifying a sale, it's your job to help your customer feel great about their decision and build a clear understanding of what it will mean for them moving forward. Continuing to put your customer and their needs first, even when you have secured their commitment to purchase, is one of the best ways you can demonstrate that you truly care about them. That's what this last step in the process is all about.

FINISH STRONG

As we discussed in the previous chapter, people would rather be unhappy than uncertain. So, now that they've committed to making a change with you, it's your job to help eliminate as much uncertainty as possible. Change and uncertainty can feel like an error to our brains and fear in our stomach, but if we understand why the change is happening and exactly what it is going to look like, we will be less likely to view it that way.

The first thing you need to do is make it completely clear to your customer that you are still with them. This is where I missed the boat when I was selling capital equipment to hospitals when I was 24 years old. So, until the change (product transaction, install, or delivery) is being applied and improvement in the customer's life is clearly observed, continue to secure Reasons to Return and stay engaged with them. This greatly benefits them, but also you in a way that is hard to measure. You need and want your customer to use your product to its fullest. Like I said earlier, this is where you overdeliver on your promises. This is where your character is confirmed by the customer. If you move on too fast after a sale, your actions are expressing that I'm more interested in the commission from the sale than the benefits from the product. Moving on too fast will also exponentially reduce the number of referrals you'll receive. By staying consistent and continuing to be there for them, it demonstrates that you are not just there for their money.

EMOTIONAL REINFORCEMENT

Another important goal you should have during this step is to help your customer feel great about their decision. They have stepped into the vision that you helped them imagine. The vision you painted where your product is equipping them to be the hero. Now you get to help that transition and help them start seeing themselves as that hero in real-time.

You know this was the right solution for your customer, so you also know there is absolutely no reason for them to feel any buyer's regret. You truly care about them, looking forward to them experiencing the benefits, and you are happy that they've made this choice that will improve their situation. This is your chance to help them feel the same way and let the people around them witness it.

This can look different in different situations. For example, if you feel that your customer may have rushed through the purchasing process a bit, take a moment to slow down after the transaction and explore emotions with them in a positive way, as we discussed in the previous chapter. Reinforce the logic involved with their purchase to help solidify in their minds the good reasoning that went into the choice they made, so they will not look back in a few days or weeks and wonder if they had missed any red flags they would have caught if they had taken more time.

Even at this point in the process, your role is to act as a guide. This isn't your moment to give your customer a lecture on all the reasons why their choice was the right choice. Stay true to the same approach you have been using throughout this process: asking good questions, listening well, allowing your customer to explore their emotions around this purchase in a way that is truly authentic to them.

It's natural to feel the instinct to try to move through this step quickly, to secure their commitment before they have any second thoughts. I can't say it enough—you're not just looking to get this one sale across the finish line. You want this change to last, and you want to continue to foster a connection with your customer that will lead to real positive change for them, loyalty and referrals over time for you.

COGNITIVE TRIGGERS

This step is all about securing your customer's commitment and creating a plan for what that commitment looks like moving forward. Obviously, commitment looks different from industry to industry based on the type of product you're selling. If you are selling something that your customer buys "off the shelf," a commitment to purchase a certain quantity of a specific product at the time of the sale, then it's usually fairly straightforward. Now, if their commitment is to start using your product on an as-needed basis, the next steps can be a little bit fuzzier. You'll be relying on them to reach out and order your product when they need it, and even if their commitment is solid, it's only as strong as their memory of you and your product. Picture a scenario where they are extremely busy and stressed out. Will they remember their commitment to you or will they, by habit, and call their old vendor?

That's why you need cognitive triggers. Cognitive triggers are psychological calls to action that will make your customer think of you and your product when familiar situations come up. For example, imagine you left your interior lights on in your car and needed a jump. Just to make sure it was the light and not a dead battery, you take your car to a repair shop to have your battery checked. The shop owner tells you, "Your battery is right on the line of weak and acceptable. You don't need a new battery just yet, but I would keep an ear on it. When you hear the car start to crank a fraction more slowly or the dash lights dim when you try to start it, come back and see me for a new battery. I'll get you in right away. I want to make sure you don't end up stranded." This shop owner just created a cognitive trigger in your mind for that particular situation. Not only will you be more apt to pick up on these subtle indicators, but you will immediately think about getting over to the shop ASAP. Even if you were not set on buying from him, his cognitive trigger has you thinking of him and might subconsciously bring you back to him.

This is your goal—to plant a seed in your customers' minds that will make them think of you when something similar happens. Your cognitive trigger needs to be specific enough that when it happens, they will immediately think of you ("Wow, I remember them mentioning this exact thing"), but it also needs to be broad enough to cover a wide spectrum of problems or situations and not be so limited that it may never happen at all.

We all have natural cognitive triggers in our day-to-day that we put in place for different reasons without even realizing it. Think about it in your own life for a moment. What level does your car's gas gauge need to get to for you to realize it is time to fill up the tank? What lets you know that it's time to go grocery shopping—an almost empty milk jug, an empty egg crate, or when the fridge just seems like it has too much free space inside? How long does your hair have to get before you decide it's time to schedule a haircut? It's your job to create new cognitive triggers like these that will help your customer's mind jump to you and your product when they need it.

Lost the sale? Cognitive triggers are even more important if you don't close the sale, if you have done everything you could do and it's time to move on. Cognitive triggers are a long-term strategy to use if a customer is not quite ready to commit to a product that you know will truly help them. Or on the other side of that scenario, you may be protecting and advising the customer to postpone the purchase, like slightly worn tires that don't need replacing, but you do not want the elderly couple to forget about it before the shallow tread leads to hydroplaning. I believe cognitive triggers are extremely powerful and helpful for all of us in all aspects of our lives! So, before moving on to the next sale, in addition to asking for a referral, make sure to leave them with something to remember, leave them with a solid cognitive trigger. You have a connection with them; make sure you protect it with a cognitive trigger that will prompt them to call you and rekindle that connection when they're ready, so you can help them to make their life better by buying from you.

Life insurance is a great example of this. If you are selling life insurance and your customer doesn't want to commit to purchasing a policy even after you have explored all the ways it could benefit them and their loved ones, you can leave them with a cognitive trigger that will help reinforce their need for your product even when they are not with you. "The next time you make a mortgage payment, take a moment to think about what might happen if you were not there to make the next payment. Would your family be able to make that payment without you?" The goal here is never to manipulate. Authenticity is always key. If you truly believe your customer will benefit from your product, placing a cognitive trigger like this can help them see that benefit in real-time.

You can tweak these to suit your needs and your customers, but here are a few examples of cognitive triggers to get you started:

Cognitive triggers for recurring purchases

- **Physical Therapist to Patient**: "Now, I really need you to hear me on this. Every time a friend or family member sees you getting up out of a chair slowly with a pained look on your face and asks, 'What's wrong? Are you okay?', I want you to call us right then and schedule an appointment."
- **Pharmaceutical Rep to Physician**: "I know you like to start all your patients on Drug X, and I totally understand why. But would you be open to prescribing Drug Z for patients who specifically mention that Drug X wears off just a little too soon and they share with you that they don't want to take another dose because it will keep them up all night?" (This might sound like you're only asking for a small sale, but in reality this is the number one complaint about Drug X, and patients commonly describe it exactly as you did, reinforcing the cognitive trigger.)
- **Meal Catering Owner to Physician Office Staff**: "Next time you have a new pharmaceutical rep requesting time with your doc, give them my

card. I'll make sure everyone is happy with their favorite dishes, and you know I'll take care of everyone's dietary needs."

- **Repair Business Owner to Customer**: "It seems that you always notice the computer running slow a day or two before it crashes, and you end up losing hours of work. So, use that slow processing speed as a trigger to call us. We'll get someone on the phone or out to see you immediately to prevent the crash and, more importantly, save your work. So, when you see the thinking wheel on the screen, think of me and call us ASAP."
- **Financial Advisor to Client:** "Next time you get a paycheck that's a little bigger than normal and makes you smile, call me, and let's see if we can't at least take a quarter of that hard-earned extra income and make it go to work for you in the smartest way possible."
- **Automotive Repair Service Writer to Customer:** "The second your car replicates that weird noise, take a mental note of your speed and what road you're on. Then call our shop, and one of us will add that information into your profile notes. Then we can see if you have time to bring it to us, so we can find this small problem before it turns into a big one."

Cognitive triggers for sales you were unable to close in the moment

- **Virus Protection Software:** "The next time you open an email that says, 'Your account is locked' or "We need to update your billing information", please contact me so we can get this software on your desktop immediately and stop anyone from viewing any of your valuable data or banking info."

- **Solar Panel Roof**: "Next time you're holding your electric bill in your hand and you wonder why it's so much higher than this month last year, call us. I'll come back out and give you another $100 off of an install proposal."
- **Real Estate Agent:** "Call me the next time you get handed a home repair invoice that turns your stomach. I will email you right away with some listings of low-maintenance homes with lower insurance and utility costs. We can also explore the option of renting your home, or share some sales comps with you. If you have a friend that is in the same situation, feel free to give them my number. I'll help them out, too; just tell them to let me know they are your friend."
- **Medical Device Rep to Surgeon:** "Would you consider using 'Implant X' on your more active patients because of the warranty and data supporting its longevity? One of your peers told me whenever a patient starts their sentence with, 'I just want to be able to do [activity] again,' he uses that as a reminder to himself to use 'Implant X.'"
- **Fiber Optic Internet Sales:** "When you're watching a movie and it starts buffering in the middle of a good scene, please text me right then, no matter the time. I will find you a promo code

to save you money and get you faster internet ASAP."

Once you've laid out a clear road map for your customer, helped reinforce their decision emotionally, and placed cognitive triggers, take a moment to celebrate; you have made it to the end of the SALES process! You have made the sale, and now you need to make sure your product is delivering on your promises. Ensuring your customer's expectations have been met. A fun and rewarding matrix to measure customer satisfaction is to track the number of referrals you receive from each sale. Talk about a powerful matrix that will hold you accountable to each customer.

CHAPTER 12
STAY AUTHENTIC

WHEN I WAS A KID, I LOVED PLAYING TENNIS WITH MY DAD. We started playing together when I was just nine years old, and I was pretty good for being so young. My dad had one trick he would use on me over and over. After a few volleys, he'd hit a shot that would bait me into the middle of the court, and on his next shot, he'd hit the ball right at me, drilling me with it and winning the point. Do not worry; he didn't hit it hard enough to leave lasting bruises.

Every time I got hit in the middle of the court, my dad would yell, "No man's land!" There are different approaches to playing tennis that can work depending on your strengths and weaknesses as a player. You might play all the way forward at the net or all the way back along the baseline. Either way, as an amateur, the middle of the court is the last place you want to firmly plant your feet. Trying to split the difference and refusing to commit to one or the other puts you at a significant disadvantage. Plus, as I learned, it might get you drilled with a tennis ball then laughed at.

This has been a lifelong lesson for me and a mantra that

I apply to several areas of my life. You can go all in and be aggressive, playing up by the net, or you can play it more conservatively and stick to the baseline. There is no wrong answer, as long as you are being true to yourself, but the takeaway is that you have to be aware of your actions, decide what path you want to take, and own it. Playing in the middle ground will not get you anywhere.

This is, of course, as true in sales as it is anywhere else. We've walked through a detailed sales process together over the last five chapters that will set you up for success if you use it well with your customers. But there is one element that is missing: you. The principles behind this sales process will be similar no matter who uses it. But the way it is put into practice should look very different from person to person.

Every step of this process offers you the opportunity to make it your own. It's the reason I named this process *Authentic* SALES, and as you discover what it looks like for you, it will help you unlock the true power behind this sales approach, the power to build trust with your customers through authenticity using an approach that is sustainable because it is true to you.

Rich Clementi, who I mentioned earlier, had no previous medical experience, unless you count the medical attention he received or witnessed as he sent other people to receive it throughout his career of seventy pro fights, thirteen of those in the UFC. When the opportunity to step into medical sales presented itself, he seized it; experience or not, he was going to win.

After about a year of submerging himself in this very technical industry, learning as much as he could about surgeons and the various therapies, he realized just showing up early and having all the needed equipment was not really bringing value. This is about the time Rich changed up his approach. He started to find his stride and be himself: an individual with no fear who always moves forward looking for ways to bring value. He quickly understood the importance of sharing best practices, discussing outcomes, and educating customers about new industry findings. He also observed, just having a superior product will not initiate change; you must share knowledge. Around this time, Rich had already witnessed firsthand over fifty patients get their lives back thanks to the physicians who selected his therapy. He used these amazing stories and interesting best practices as conversation starters with physicians who cared about the therapy. Several people warned him that he was too "blunt" in his sales approach, but he chose to stick with it, staying true to who he was.

Rich's "Business First" conversation approach turned off one or two physicians out of the forty he called on. The rest of them look forward to seeing him and view his approach as being real. They enjoy his energy and love his passion toward the industry. Talk to him for five minutes, and you will see how much he believes in his product and how it changes lives. The physicians that work with him see his passion, his commitment to their patients' outcomes, and the work he puts into making sure everything is perfect in this high-stakes field of medicine. They understand that this is a guy they are lucky to have in their corner. It took some time and maybe a few "black eyes," but Rich stayed true to himself. He embraced the freedom to approach sales in a way that felt authentic to him, and it wasn't long before he was on fire as a sales rep.

Early in my sales career, I realized that one of my biggest fears was failure. That's a challenging place to be as a sales rep because failure is inherently part of the job; you have to be willing to fail if you're going to succeed. I decided to employ that self-awareness and use my fear to my advantage. I didn't try to "fix" myself or try to deny the fear I felt. I used it as motivation to get better, to practice a few extra times, knock on a few more doors, or devote extra time to research and preparation. It turned into a driving force, not because I eliminated it, but because I was willing to accept it as part of who I was.

You already have everything you need to become a successful sales professional. You can grow in your skills, of course. You can practice, you can learn, and you can gain experience and wisdom over time that will help you to improve. But you do not need to change who you are as a person and try to become someone you are not. You just need to know yourself well enough to figure out how to tailor this process to fit your own strengths and weaknesses.

The reason I created this sales process was to help people adopt and implement proven steps in a way that is true to them. So, take what you have learned in this book and figure out what it looks like for you. Be yourself all the way. Never, ever apologize for being who you are.

FAILURE IS NOT THE END

The hardest part of sales comes down to one word: "rejection." Sometimes even just the anticipation of rejection is even harder, especially when you are prospecting. We're all driven individuals who want to succeed, and if you truly care about the people you are selling to and want to help them, the thought of them rejecting you can produce a lot of stress and anxiety.

That being said, I believe we're going about this all wrong. Experienced hunters do not kill everything they encounter, but they love what they do. Professional fishermen have a low percentage of casts versus the fish they turn in at the end of a tournament, but they love what they do. Why? Because what looks like failure to the untrained eye is actually them being selective. They are picking their moments so that when they do experience a win, it will be the *right* win.

The moment you decide to be selective in your approach to sales, you will see your situation in a whole new light. Failure will feel less like failure because if a customer decides you are not the right rep for them, there's a good chance they're not the right customer for you, either. It takes a bit more time and patience, but thinking about succeeding with the *right* customers will help you to build the kind of customer base you want over time, customers that you can serve in the way they deserve to be served. Practice this, and it will reduce anxiety.

Of course, there are times when we will experience failure that is just straight-up failure. It's part of life, and it's a big part of sales. But failure doesn't have to be all negative. The best time to look for a new opportunity is when you are getting back up.

I competed in MMA for several years, and in preparation for a local fight at a new higher-weight class, I started pushing a little harder with my sparring. This led to the only time I was ever knocked out. It happened right after I had dropped a sparring partner to his knee; he bounced right back up and knocked me out. Instead of worrying about recovering, he noticed me admiring my achievement with my hands down and recognized his opportunity. He may have been in a disadvantaged position, but he saw an opening, capitalized on it, and taught me a lesson.

When the stock market crashes, 90% of people are looking to just stop their losses. While the great investors, those with experience, know that it's time to look for good deals. When I land in a new country and get in the car with a local rep, a common question I ask them is, "Who's the most confident rep you compete against, and which of their accounts do they spend the least amount of time in?" For an industry with recurring sales, these accounts are usually the low-hanging fruit. They might have been considered "losses" for these reps at one point, but if they are willing to get up, keep fighting, and create a solid strategy, they can turn into wins that will change the momentum of their entire sales territory.

If you're creative, observant, and opportunistic enough, you can even find wins by taking advantage of someone else's momentum. In some industries, when one company's customer finally tries a competitor's product for the first time, their loyalty to "product A" has been symbolically broken. The competitive rep offering "product B" either worked hard to break into the account or just happened to be in the right place at the right time. Either way, the door is now open, not just to them, but to anyone. If you are selling "product C," you can seize the moment and join the party, looking for ways to get the customer to try your product before a new habit is formed with "product B."

When we look back on hard times we've gone through, we like to brag about them like they're badges of honor. They've helped us to grow, and often, they preceded an opportunity of some kind. So, why not take perspective even in the midst of the hard times? It might feel strange to think about enjoying it when things aren't going your way.

Find purpose in the pain, make the best of it, strap in, take notes, and understand this is going to help you grow. We all learn more from our losses than we do from our wins.

Here's a cognitive trigger for you. When you find yourself unsure of how to rekindle a conversation with a prospect, or you're about to leave a voicemail that goes, "I was just calling to check in and see if you've reviewed the proposal I sent," pause and think of me with a smile. Instead of proceeding, circle back to chapter seven and refresh your memory with "Reasons to Return." Keep your spirits high; such situations are common, even for the best of us.

In the grand journey of your sales career, setbacks are mere footnotes eclipsed by the strength of your determination. Nothing external can dim the fire of your drive. If you come equipped with unwavering resolve, embrace hard work, and remain steadfast in bouncing back from setbacks—all while staying true to who you are—then success isn't a mere possibility; it's your destiny. As you close this book, remember that the ultimate goal is conquering your own limitations. Forge ahead and be unstoppable.

AFTERWORD

My hope is that the time we spent together as you read this book has been similar to the time you will now spend with your customers as you use this method. I have tried to practice what I have been preaching. I have done my best throughout this book to implement the 80/20 rule, focusing on painting a picture of all the positive things that can happen for you if you use this method well. I have tried to give you interesting and meaningful information in various forms—stories, research, examples of what these principles look like in practice—to give you valuable information throughout the book.

More than anything, I have written this book because I care about you. I am sharing this method because I know it works, and I believe it can make a difference in your career as a sales professional. In my heart, I want the best for every person who reads this book, the very same way you want the best for every customer you sell to.

When you find yourself in a difficult situation, come back to this book. Remind yourself of the principles. Reflect on the principles that make this method work and the steps that make it work. If you have a friend or colleague who's struggling, give them this book. If they are in a funk, my advice would be to start in the section on NOW goals and then read the rest of the book.

You're ready now to put this into practice. So go do it. Stay true to yourself. Care deeply about your customers. Use this book as your field manual, your guide to building trust and connecting. More than anything, be authentic, be you. Everything you need to execute this sales process successfully is already inside you. Accept that as truth, and you'll be on your way to making a real difference in the lives of your customers and your loved ones.

ACKNOWLEDGMENTS

To my amazing wife, Stacy, who has always believed in me, sensing that greater things lay ahead and urging me beyond my own limitations. Thank you for your unfailing love, encouragement, support, sacrifices, and for showing me grace even when I imperfectly placed work ahead of our relationship. I love you! You are and will always be my Lil One.

To my parents: Dad, thank you for your character and your teachings. I do things the correct way because of you. By the way, I was actually listening. Mom, thank you for your encouragement, and for always fighting for me to have an opportunity even when I didn't deserve it.

To my three boys: Thank you, Diesel, for inspiring me to be the best I can be and to go back to school. Your strength, faith, and dedication have motivated me to become a better version of myself. Thank you, Axle, for helping me be authentic and lean into my creativity. Thank you, John Steel, for keeping me young and giving me another opportunity to raise a Godly young man.

Thank you to all the men in my life who believed in me, spoke life into me, and took the time to listen when needed. You know who you are: my brother, brothers, small group, teammates, colleagues, and friends.

ACKNOWLEDGMENTS

ABOUT THE AUTHOR

Founder of **Q3 Consulting and Coaching**, Travis McCoy isn't just a sales strategist and coach; he has lived and breathed sales for decades. As a collegiate athlete at SLU, Travis began his sales journey selling; autos, security systems, mortgages, financial services, capital equipment, and medical devices, and shattering records at all of them, including two Fortune 500 companies. His journey is nothing short of inspiring. Recognized as a 10x "President's Club" winner, "Rep of the Year" and highest annual revenue producer for seven years (with territory cut six times). Internationally, Travis made his mark in 42 countries across five continents and played pivotal roles in launching new products and consulting startups across various industries. Now, as a coveted sales consultant and coach, Travis's extensive expertise and passionate approach make him an unmatched guide for those looking for serious growth.

Made in the USA
Las Vegas, NV
19 January 2024

84611411R00163